Watermark
Guide to
Fishing in
Kansas

Watermark Guide to Fishing in Kansas

George Stanley

Watermark
Press

799.1
stan

Watermark Press, Inc.
149 North Broadway, Suite 201
Wichita, Kansas 67202

ISBN 0-922820-14-7

Cover and interior design:
ACME DESIGN COMPANY
JOHN BAXTER, MICHAEL KLINE

Cover illustration:
JACQUI MORGAN

Photographs by MIKE BLAIR: 4, 7, 8, 9, 10, 16, 22, 23
(top left), 39, 41, 66, 72, 134. © Kansas Wildlife
and Parks.

Photographs by GENE BREHM: 23 (bottom left), 30,
32, 44, 46, 54, 56, 57, 58, 61, 76, 134, 144, 146.
© Kansas Wildlife and Parks.

Photographs by MICHAEL SOLURI: 19 (jig, plastic
worm), 20 (spinnerbait, crankbait, spinner,
spoon), 21 (topwater lure) © Michael Soluri

Photograph by JOEL SARTORE: 165 © Joel Sartore

Illustrations by KAY HOLMES STAFFORD: 36 (largemouth bass), 42 (smallmouth bass), 48 (walleye),
52 (striped bass), 56 (white bass), 62 (black crappie), 63 (bluegill, yellow perch), 69 (channel catfish), 70 (flathead catfish). © Kay Holmes
Stafford.

FIRST PRINTING

Thank you to my teachers — the out-
doorsmen who introduced me to the lakes
and streams of Kansas. They start with
Steve Harper, my Flint Hills fishing part-
ner and successor on the *Wichita Eagle*
outdoors beat. Special thanks as well to
Elden Bailey, Bruce Coate, Mike Cox,
Kurt Geis, Bill Harmon, Mike Hayden,
Ron Hopkins, Mike Miller, Michael
Pearce and Jim Reid.

Most of all, I would like to thank my
wife Pam for her patience, support, inspiration and love.

— *George Stanley*

Section Three
H$_2$O

To Jim Stanley, who taught me how to tie a hook, cast a lure and clean a fish. He often said he didn't have the patience to be a good fisherman. Yet he somehow found time to spend many long, quiet hours on the water, building memories with his son.

THIS BOOK IS my attempt to write the guide I'd like to read as a Kansas fisherman. Focusing on waters, species and weather specific to the state, it's a guide that describes how the moods, foods, hangouts and habits of gamefish fluctuate with the seasons. 🐟 Lures, baits, gear and techniques that have proven most effective on Kansas ponds, lakes and streams are discussed in detail. Maps explain what fish habitat looks like and where to find it. A map of each major reservoir is included, featuring key fish holding areas. Descriptions of all public waters in the state, including streams, rivers, state lakes and city ponds are provided. Maps pinpoint the location of public access points. The state's top bass, walleye, striper, catfish, crappie and panfish anglers share their expertise, as well as some of their favorite fishing stories. State fisheries biologists detail what they know about the waters they manage. 🐟 In addition, I have tried, throughout the book, to pass on a bit of my love for the natural beauty of one of America's best-kept secrets: the Kansas outdoors.

Happy Fishing,
George Stanley

Kansas, the Best-Kept Secret in the Midwest

Simon Peter said
unto them, 'I go a fishing.'
They said unto him, 'We
also go with thee.'
JOHN 21-3

GOD NEVER MADE a lake in Kansas, it is said. It's also said that every hour spent fishing will be added to your life. Perhaps dreams of immortality made Kansans work like beavers to dam up the state's streams and rivers, forming 25 major reservoirs, more than 100 state and community lakes, and countless farm ponds and watershed pools.

Today, silver striped bass swim in a reservoir thousands of miles from their native Atlantic, cruising along country roads now buried under 50 feet of backed-up river. The underwater roadways — still flanked by fallen trees and postrock pillars — crisscross at square-mile section lines. There, walleye, crappie and other fish search for food among the twisted branches of forgotten fencerows.

Elsewhere on the impoundment, a hen wood duck squeals and flies overhead as a fisherman flips lures toward the dead trunks of cottonwoods and sycamores which once lined a creek and still mark its channel. In deeper water, white bass herd a school of shad to the surface, drawing swooping seagulls down from above, whooping like cowboys at roundup time.

Along shore, a father and son sit in the shade, waiting for their bobbers to sink with the weight of a bluegill, catfish or whatever happens by. They are fishing, more than anything else, for memories. Already they've hooked the time when the boy, at the ripe age of 4, ran a big channel cat onto the bank after his push-button reel broke. And the time a black bass exploded on the surface, flipping and jumping all the way in, before finally shaking free at the last second — a 7-pounder for sure! Mostly, they've caught quiet, lazy afternoons filled with long, gentle conversations.

Through the years, those memories remain — tossing, drifting, sailing through the mind — the gifts of time well-spent. All it takes to bring them back is the lip-lap of waves against a dock, a whiff of sweet cedar in the breeze, or maybe just that outboard smell of oil-in-gas.

This book is intended to be nothing more or less than a tool for building memories. You won't find a lot in here about the hot lures of the year. But you should find a good deal about the habits and haunts of the gamefish species that share your favorite waters, whether you like to drift a reservoir for channel catfish, fly-cast for green sunfish in a Flint Hills stream, or slip a little bass boat into a pond left behind by miners, as a beaver slaps the water and a cardinal trills from the trees.

Though often overlooked, Kansas boasts as many raw materials for outdoor memory making as any other place in America, south of Alaska. It's the best kept secret in the Midwest.

Each day, thousands of Interstate highway travelers race across Kansas, finding nothing Great about her Plains — just a yawning breadth of flatland that hinders their hurry to crowded coasts and claustral mountains. How far they are from the nature of this place, where four winds swirl through dramatic skies that stretch out from horizon to horizon, unobstructed by smog, skyscrapers, or trees.

It is the dearth of trees that many find monotonous — an irony, since it is the prairie's wild and unpredictable nature that discourages long-lived, immobile plants from taking root. To make it on the plains, you've got to roll with the wind or get out of its way. Tough trees, like cottonwoods, hunker in draws and cling to life-bearing streams. Less hardy varieties wither after a few weeks without water, becoming tinder for a lightning bolt or grass fire.

Rain eventually falls on the ashes left by the pasture fires of spring. Up pops a wavy sea of green grasses flecked with white, blue, purple, pink, red, orange and yellow wildflowers. Bees and butterflies flit among flowers as grasshoppers nibble at the greenery. Prairie chicks chase down insect meals as deer bed in grass that reaches higher than a buffalo's eye.

Clear streams flow through valleys between the gentle hills of green. Broad-winged shadows circle across the waters as turkey vultures rise and soar on morning thermals. Croaking bullfrogs, hammering woodpeckers and clucking wild turkeys add rhythm to the drone of cicadas in the trees.

Against all of this background music, a pair of fishermen shuffle through the grass toward a small pond encircled by large, flat rocks. Blue asters and blazing yellow clumps of broomweed speck the hills. A breeze carries the sweet smell of sage — piquant perfume of the Flint Hills. Clouds drift northward across a deep blue sky as the anglers rig up plastic worms, cast them

out, then dance them back across the pond bottom.

Splash! A fin breaks the surface, a rod twitches. Splash! The fish leaves the water before making one last run. The first bass of the day weighs in at nearly three pounds.

"My wife doesn't understand why I drive an hour just to go fishing," one of the fishermen says, releasing his large-mouth. "I don't understand why she doesn't. It's like the dedication in a book I've got at home: 'To my father, who taught me to love hot chili and to understand those who don't.'"

After catching several dozen bass in three ponds, the partners head at dusk to a kettle-shaped hollow filled with clear spring water: their favorite fishing hole. It is nestled in the hills like a pearl in an oyster. As evening falls, the oyster opens its shell for a glorious view of the sky.

A towering cumulus cloud glows in the twilight, matching the ghostly white of shoreline boulders. As minnows flip out of the mirror calm shallows in fright, the anglers toss lures past the commotion, then reel back through, taking two bass with every three casts. They hardly notice the dark settling in, until the lures become invisible. Then they follow their progress by sound — a splash as spinnerbait hits the water, a crash as it meets the rod tip.

Casting now toward the sound of plops instead of the sight of ripples, the fisher-

men walk separately along the bank. Even the noise of sneakers against earth, of pants against leg, sounds loud. When one angler stumbles over a cow track in the dried mud and slaps his rod against a rock, the noise seems almost deafening.

Cricket music eventually replaces the harsh cicada whines. A freight train rumbles across distant tracks, never blowing its whistle. A great-horned owl clears its chest with a series of hoots. The fishermen rarely speak, and then only in whispers.

Billions of stars sparkle overhead, brilliant against the dark night of a new moon. Constellations reflect in the still, black water. Glow worms — firefly larvae that keep their tail lights on, afraid to blink — dot the rocks along shore. It's hard to tell where sky ends and earth begins.

"Everything pales by comparison to the universe; I can't even begin to grasp it," a fisherman says, looking straight up.

Yet the stars seem closer in these hills; the expanse above looks more like a window than a vacuum.

Many times in history, God has whispered in the ears of fishermen, shepherds and others who spend long, quiet hours with the night sky. Or perhaps He speaks to everyone, but the readers of the night are in a better position to listen?

Whatever the answer, there is something about fishing that is good for the soul. And while Kansas isn't sprinkled with glacial lakes or mountain streams, it has been blessed with plenty of places to wet a line and contemplate the finer mysteries of life.

L IKE EVERYTHING ELSE, fishing nowadays seems far more complicated than it used to. A friend at a party once mentioned that he would like to try fishing sometime. He was married with two children; his hairline was receding. "But I've never been fishing before," he said. "I don't even know where to start."

As America's population has become more urban, fewer folks have grown up like Tom Sawyer, fishpole in hand. Meanwhile, a huge industry has wound itself around sport fishermen, constantly generating new rods, reels, lures, lines, motors, boats, accessories and gimmicks. Every improvement in materials or technology spawns books, videos and magazine articles insinuating you can't catch fish without it.

Suddenly fishing — long among the most relaxing and least intimidating of pastimes — seems as confusing and troublesome as computer science to the inexperienced.

Actually, catching fish can be easier today than it has ever been, presuming you ply waters that still support aquatic life. Today's standard tools — from boats to bobbers, trailers to trolling motors — generally work better than the best available equipment of 10, 20 or 30 years ago.

Yet the old stuff and old ways will still catch fish. In fact, a cane pole, a few feet of line and a hook still add up to a great starting rig, especially for a young child.

Many of today's top fishermen got their start by simply finding a worm under a streamside rock and tossing it to a fishy looking place — say, a deep hole along a bend. They let the bait settle to the bottom, took the slack out of the line, leaned back against a tree trunk and relaxed. Sooner or later, something sucked up the worm, tugged on the line and got itself yanked onto the bank.

That first catch taught the fisherman that a certain type of bait (worm) would trick a certain type of fish (bass) in a certain type of place (shady pool with sunken brush) on a certain kind of day (warm and sunny).

On other days in other places, the angler learned that other baits would catch other species. An expert fishermen simply has figured out enough about fish hangouts, moods and favorite foods to enjoy success most times out.

He may know, for instance, that crappie head to brushy shallows in springtime, where they'll attack anything resembling a minnow.

Meanwhile, walleye will congregate in shallow, rocky places, such as dams and points, that feature current or wave action. There, they will nail minnows, minnow-lures and nightcrawlers.

About the same time of year, largemouth bass will start heading up creek

channels into warm shallow water, then hug up against a tree trunk, a brushpile, a cut in the bank. They'll often ambush slow-moving objects, including crankbaits and spinnerbaits, while attacking threatening intruders, such as plastic eels and heavy jigs with pork-rind tails.

"Some of these TV guys make it seem so complicated, like you've got to start with $70,000 worth of stuff and go from there," says Elden Bailey, one of Kansas' top anglers. "All you've got to do is throw a worm in the water. Of course, it does help to know where."

All in all, sport fishing fundamentals really haven't changed much since Izaak Walton wrote the first great English-language guidebook for fishermen in 1653. In *The Compleat Angler* Walton offered poetic praise of "piscators" while explaining where and how one should present worms, frogs, flies and other live and artificial baits.

In Walton's day, fishing was mechanically simple, profoundly relaxing and a trifle mysterious — "the contemplative man's recreation."

At its best, fishing remains all of this today.

A youngster lowers a worm into the water and waits. Something yanks his line, jerks his rod and he reels, reels, reels, not knowing what he's fighting — bass, crappie, walleye, catfish — until he pulls it from the water (if he pulls it from the water).

"God didn't intend for us to talk to those fish, and if He did, it would take all the fun out of it," said Bailey, a two-time state walleye champion. "I don't want to get too scientific because I enjoy the mysteries."

BOTTOM READERS
That's not to say that Bailey ignores technological advances that can expand his knowledge of a body of water, enabling him to better apply his long-earned understanding of fish and how to catch them.

He routinely scans lakes with a depthfinder, mapping structural variations, or "edges," that attract fish. River and creek channels are usually the most important landmark edges to locate, followed by dropoffs, points, humps or hills, ledges, sunken islands, trees and brushpiles.

As useful as sonar eyes can be, however, a depthfinder is by no means a requirement for successful reservoir fishing. In fact, the depthfinder broke down during one of my most enjoyable trips to Wilson Reservoir, the deepest lake in Kansas. In place of sonar, we had a detailed map of the lake and a companion who fished there so many times he could point out marks on the map that were "a little bit off."

Putting in around sunrise at a state park boat ramp, we headed west to a point at the mouth of Nelson Cove. About 40 yards offshore — directly facing a buoy that served as our landmark — we jigged slab spoons in 12 feet of water. Within moments, we were tangling with scrappy two-pound white bass that slammed our jigs as we snapped them off the bottom.

Experienced readers of depth finders, topographic maps and shorelines will often detect other fish hideouts, such as gravel roads, rockpiles and railroad beds. If you see where an old gravel road comes up to the lake and stops, for example, chances are fair that the path continues underwater to the other side. Sink a jig to the bottom and slowly reel it in, trying to feel the bump-bump-bump of a lure bouncing off gravel. Often bordered by trees, brush and ditches, old roads are favorite highways for walleye, wipers, stripers and other species.

By talking to local experts and looking up old maps, a serious fisherman can learn the location of bridge pilings, fenceposts, building foundations, and old dams for stock ponds and small lakes that were consumed with the flooding of the reservoir.

"In Kansas, where there is limited structure, you look for anything that's different," says Haysville bass pro Randy Stovall.

Gamefish seem to be attracted to structures simply because they are there, as points of reference, even when they don't offer an abundance of food, cover or shade.

After an hour of non-stop action on big whites at Nelson Cove, we crossed the lake to Lucas Point and began trolling over the most structurally diverse area of lake bottom, hoping to find stripers there.

Traveling about two knots in the cool fall weather, we were trailing black-and-silver minnow lures, kept suspended at 18 feet deep by downrigger weights. When nothing hit after a few passes, we left for another potential hot spot: Rocktown Cove. A pocket of rugged beauty in the barren Smoky Hills, the rocks of Rocktown stood like monuments sculpted by a desert wind and blazed with the colors of Indian paints — yellow, orange, flaming red. Stunted trees, their roots exposed, clung to the shelter of crevices in the rocks.

A large flight of shorebirds rolled like a wave in the sky and then spiraled out of sight beyond a distant point. A seagull lilted by. We ate sandwiches and sipped pop.

Suddenly, a pole snapped to attention, line buzzing off the reel.

A striper had taken the lure, snapping the rubber band that connected the fishing line to the heavy downrigger weight. Once released of the weight, the bowed rod straightened up, automatically setting the hook. Now, the rod bounced with the fight of the fish.

Before we had the first rod out of its stern-mounted holder, a second pole sprang to life. We landed twin stripers, each weighing about 5 pounds. The action continued for two more hours, the stripers usually hitting in pairs.

You don't need a big boat and down-rigger equipment to enjoy reservoir fishing either, though guided trips can be an excellent way to learn about unfamiliar waters.

At most Kansas lakes, you can drift calm nights away in nothing larger than a canoe and consistently catch limits of channel catfish.

Walleye, crappie and largemouth bass often come within easy reach of shore in spring and fall. In cold winters, when thick ice forms on the big lakes, you can walk out, make holes with a hand-augur or spud, and enjoy spectacular white bass fishing in many reservoirs.

LAND-LOCKED

Using rods and reels designed for saltwater surf fishing, some anglers now cast cut bait hundreds of feet from reservoir points to river channels that are cruised year-round by stripers, catfish, walleye and whites.

Wading out from the points into waist-deep water, the fishermen heave out their heavy-weighted lines, then slowly reel out more line while returning to shore. They anchor their long fishing poles in the sand, then watch as the rods wave in the wind like saplings on the beach.

There's no mistaking when a striper hits — the rod tip bounces frantically. Even a small striper provides great sport with hundreds of feet of line out. Often, fish have to be skillfully steered away from shoreline brush before they can be guided to the beach.

Chet Nily of Sylvan Grove wasn't even using big saltwater equipment on a May night in 1988, when he cast a small white bass, as bait, off Wilson Reservoir's Lucas Point.

Half-an-hour later, he sat on the beach and tried to catch his breath after winning a 15-round knockout against a heavy-weight striper. Nily donated his 43½ pound state record to the Kansas Department of Wildlife and Parks; it is now on display in the state Conservation Education Center below the Milford Reservoir Dam.

Even shorefishing can be tremendously sophisticated. Izaak Walton covered it exclusively in his book, and a good deal has been learned by European bank fishermen in the three centuries since. Using European equipment, purchased mostly through catalogs, Wichita psychiatrist Mike Keyes and his sons enjoy spectacular success on panfish, catfish and carp in hard-fished city park waters.

Their tools include very long, sensitive poles, lightweight lines, dainty hooks and an array of streamlined balsa bobbers — some for rough water, others for calm, some for casting, others for pitching, some to keep bait shallow, others to hold it deep.

As the slim floats dip down, Keyes simply tilts his long fishing pole up and swings the fish on a pendulum to hand. "This place is heavily fished and no one catches anything," he said one evening on the bank at Watson Park Lake, in the middle of Wichita. "We come down here and catch 100 bluegill in a couple hours."

Kansas fly fishermen enjoy excellent fishing for panfish, stream bass, farmpond largemouths, even carp. With a modern float tube and a pair of foot flippers, you could easily fish virtually all of the state's fishing lakes, community lakes, watershed lakes, farm ponds, rivers and streams without ever stepping foot in a boat. An inexpensive canoe, johnboat or molded-plastic bass raft would enable you to

DAILY LIMITS

Daily creel limits for major species are:

SPECIES	LIMIT
Black bass	5*
Bluegill, sunfish	NO LIMIT
Channel catfish	10
Crappie	NO LIMIT**
Flathead catfish	5
Stripers	2
Walleye	5
White bass	NO LIMIT
Wipers	2

*Any combination of largemouth, spotted or smallmouth.

**The Kansas Wildlife and Parks Commission was considering new creel limits on crappie when this book went to print. For an update on crappie limits, call the Wildlife and Parks operations headquarters in Pratt at (316) 672-5911.

safely and efficiently cover about every piece of water except the major reservoirs, and you could bite off chunks of them as well.

SAY PLEASE

Of course, most of the state's prettiest streams and liveliest ponds aren't open to the public without permission. All but three percent of Kansas is private property — the nation's highest ratio of private to public land.

Unlike many states, which allow people to walk on unposted property, Kansas law prohibits trespassing without permission, whether or not there are "No Trespassing" signs. If signs are present, you can be ticketed unless you produce written permission from the landowner — even if the landowner says you don't need it.

While the water in Kansas creeks and rivers belongs to the public, adjacent landowners own and control the banks and stream bed, except along the navigable Kansas, Arkansas and Missouri Rivers.

Legally speaking, this means you can float on any stream in Kansas without permission, so long as you enter and exit at public access points and don't step out of the water and onto private land anywhere in between. Practically speaking, you should ask permission first.

"I ran some fellows off the stream last week," a Flint Hills rancher told a friend and me after giving us permission to fish on his stream and several of his ponds. "The fishing doesn't bother me. Even if everyone fished out here they couldn't catch 15 percent of them. But those fellows didn't ask permission. They were fishing on land that I lease out for $10,000 — and there were a lot of cattle out there."

Ask and you will usually receive, says Pratt sportsman Mike Cox, whose abstract map of Pratt County landowners is quilted with yellows squares and rectangles of three different sizes. Each yellow shape indicates square-mile sections, half-sections and quarter sections on which Cox has permission to hunt and fish.

Cox fishes for bass on a spring-fed stream and several farm ponds lying just a few miles from his home in town. In moist years, he enjoys excellent duck hunting on a beaver pond near his office. He has permission to hunt pheasant, turkey, quail and deer on 15 landowners' fields and pastures.

He didn't have access to any private land in the county when a job promotion brought him to Pratt. Shortly after coming to town, Cox bought a map from a local abstract company that showed who owned the surrounding countryside. When he spotted an attractive spot, he checked his map, then searched nearby mailboxes for the landowner's name.

"Sometimes it takes a lot of footwork," he said. "A lot of times you find the landowner leases the ground. Generally, he'll leave it up to the lessee whether to give you permission or not So you go through the same process with the lessee."

Cox introduces himself, tells the landowner or lessee where he lives, points out the spot he's interested in and asks if he can hunt or fish there.

He asks the landowner if there are any

special restrictions or conditions, to avoid future misunderstandings. Ranchers, for example, often steer folks away from pastures holding livestock, the source of their livelihood. As a result, ponds open to a fisherman some months will be closed during others.

A landowner might want to save a privately stocked honey hole for family and special friends. He may temporarily put a pasture off limits because a dry spell has him worried that a tossed-off cigarette or hot car muffler could spark a range fire.

Cox agrees to abide by the landowner's rules. He asks whether he can bring a couple of friends along from time to time and whether the landowner wants to be contacted each time Cox plans to stop by.

"A few prefer to be called each time, but most just want to know my vehicle and where I'll park it," he said.

He tries to spread his fishing and hunting around, never visiting one landowner too many times. "You don't want to wear out your welcome by hammering the same place every weekend."

His family often camps on private lands, too. If Cox sees a nice camping spot on land where he has access to fish, he'll ask the landowner for separate permission for the new activity.

While camping, the family gathers wild plums for jelly. A jar of the jelly is often returned to the property owner, along with a loaf of home-baked bread, at Christmas. He asks if the landowner likes fish or pheasant or venison, and brings those that do an occasional filet or bird or steak. "But the homemade item around Christmas means more to them than anything else," he said.

Most ranchers will react favorably to fishermen who ask before they cast, said Mike Beam of the Kansas Livestock Association. "You should talk to the landowner and let him gain confidence in you," he said. "In return, he might give you other leads, tell you the history of the

pond — stuff that you'd never find out otherwise."

Indeed, once you get to know a landowner, he'll often invite you to fish a pond you didn't know existed, or offer himself as a reference to use when asking a neighboring farmer for permission to fish.

One evening, a fishing partner and I were standing in the yard, exchanging fish stories with a farmer, his father and a friend of the family as a seven-week-old puppy undid our shoes. The farmer's father recalled a few of his own experiences on the stream we had come to fish.

"I used to catch a lot of fish there with my brother-in-law," he said. "He always used a Lazy Ike plug and he always outfished me. Boy, I was glad when he lost that plug."

We all laughed. Later that evening, while fishing the stream, I dug up an old Lazy Ike from the bottom of the tackle box and it helped put an end to a lull in the action.

In rural areas, away from the perimeter of major cities, more than half of a polite angler's inquiries will probably gain him new places to fish. That's not all he'll gain, according to Cox. "The landowners who have given me permission are good friends now," he said.

KANSAS FISHING REGULATIONS
Are you:
☞ Under 16 years old?
☞ 65 or older?
☞ A Kansas resident on leave from the armed forces?

If you answered yes to one of the above, then you don't need a license to fish in Kansas.

Everyone else must buy a license.

Annual, five-day and one-day licenses are available for residents and nonresidents. You may also buy a combination hunting/fishing license. No special stamps are required for fishing in Kansas.

Fishing seasons are open year-round

for every major sport species and all but one or two odd minor ones (such as paddlefish). This may come as a surprise to out-of-state anglers accustomed to the rites and rigors of Opening Day. Kansas fisheries officials believe seasons aren't necessary because daily limits and length restrictions provide enough protection for the fish, even during their spawning seasons.

Length limits on black bass — largemouth, smallmouth and spotted — are posted at most lakes. The standard minimum is 15 inches. An 18-inch limit has been imposed on a few intensely fished bass waters, including El Dorado and Hillsdale reservoirs.

Some lakes feature "slot" length limits of 12-to-15 or 12-to-18 inches. On these waters, biologists think small bass must be culled to prevent overpopulation and stunted growth, while medium-sized bass must be preserved to keep panfish numbers in check. Catch a bass under 12 inches at Big Hill Reservoir, for example, and you should consider keeping it for the good of the lake. Catch a nine-pound trophy, which dwarfs the upper slot limit of 18 inches, and you can take it to the taxidermist if you wish. But catch a largemouth that measures 12½ or 17¾ inches and you must release it right away.

Measure a fish from its snout, with mouth closed, to the tip of its tail, with the lobes pressed together. That's how the game warden will do it.

A 30-inch length limit applies statewide for northern pike, which are extremely rare in Kansas. Many lakes have posted walleye length limits of 18 inches, including Cheney, Big Hill, Cedar Bluff, Melvern, El Dorado, Elk City, Hillsdale, Pomona and LaCygne Reservoirs. A 15-inch walleye limit has been imposed at Glen Elder Reservoir. Except for northern pike, there are no length limits on rivers, streams or farm ponds, unless privately imposed by a landowner or lessee.

Daily creel limits run from midnight to midnight. They apply on all streams, rivers, public lakes and reservoirs. They also apply on ponds and watershed lakes that cross property lines, and on any ponds stocked within the past 10 years by the Department of Wildlife and Parks. Creel limits do not apply on private ponds which the state has not stocked.

Species with no daily limits are protected by wanton waste regulations that prohibit people from dumping excess fish or not putting them to good use.

Each angler may have two lines. Unattended lines must be tagged with name and address. A fisherman may have one trotline or eight setlines. Each setline must have a name tag and be checked at least once every 24 hours.

Jug lines — floats with lines attached that are sometimes used for catching catfish — are illegal in Kansas. It is also unlawful to hand fish, or "noodle" catfish.

Fish cannot be kept unless hooked in the mouth. All snagged or foul-hooked fish must be released immediately.

All streambeds belong to adjoining landowners, except the legally navigable Kansas, Arkansas and Missouri rivers. Anglers must have permission to cross private property.

Fishing regulations can change from year to year. Brochures explaining current regulations and license fees are available at all Wildlife and Parks offices and any competently managed sporting goods store.

A few stores that sell fishing equipment and licenses are run by people who know nothing about the sport. I once stopped at a big discount department store in Wichita on Jan. 1 — it was one of the few places open on New Year's Day — and tried to buy a fishing license. The guy behind the sports counter told me they had run out of fishing licenses for the new year. Imagine. With only 364½ days to go!

FOLKS HAVE BEEN catching fish with hook and line since the Stone Age, and many generations of fishermen between then and now have added twists of imagination to the art of angling. These days, sport fishermen have a staggering array of tools at their disposal. ☞ You might require little more than a pole, some line and a hook to catch fish. But once hooked on the sport, your desires for more equipment seem to grow with every outing that might have gone better if you'd only had…

As a result, there always will be a few more weapons you'd like to see added to the arsenal.

For an indication of the tools which a Kansas fisherman might find most handy, here's a hypothetical wish list for an avid angler who likes to case everything from bluegills to stripers.

RODS AND REELS

☞ An ultralight spinning outfit, with spools of two-pound and four-pound test line. This would be the "fun" rod, used on everything from green sunfish to spotted bass. Preferably made of graphite, a quality graphite/fiberglass combination will do if the budget requires.

☞ A light-action, six-foot spinning rod, with spools of six and eight-pound clear, monafilament line. This is an all-around rod that'll do for most kinds of fishing, especially walleye, white bass and channel catfish.

☞ A medium-action spinning rod for trolling after walleye, whites, wipers and stripers. Add a heavy-action rod if you're serious about stripers.

☞ A sturdy 5½ or 6-foot baitcasting rod and reel, with 12 to 18-pound test line. Stiff enough to set the hook on a lunker largemouth, it also provides enough leverage to steer her away from line-snapping stumps. Enables you to make pinpoint casts of heavy lures to largemouth hideaways. The more you bass fish, the more variations you'll want of this rod and reel. Tournament bass fishermen keep several baitcasting rods, ready to go, each with a different lure. Buy the best graphite rod you can afford — sometimes only a slight vibration will tell you that a huge bass has inhaled your plastic worm, and you've got to set the hook before she spits it back out.

☞ A 7 to 8 foot flyrod, strong enough to deliver streamers to black bass, yet supple enough to land a mosquito on a redear's nose. You won't want the rod to be too long, as most casts will be short and branches hang thick and low over Kansas streams.

☞ A heavy-duty saltwater surfcasting rod with a reel that handles plenty of line. This rod will enable you to reach striper highways — old river channels — from the points along Cheney, Glen Elder and Wilson Lakes.

☞ A 14-foot telescopic "crappie" pole. Fiberglass will work fine. Add a couple yards of light line, a sensitive float, a small hook and a maggot or bit of worm, and you're set for perpetual action during the panfish spawning seasons.

☞ A medium-action spincasting rod for simple push-button fishing. With eight-pound test, it's a hard rig to beat for baitfishing, for panfish, for kids, for guests or for a worry-free second line in the water.

TACKLE

☞ First, you need a box to store your stuff in. Specialists, especially bass fishermen, tend to keep several tackle boxes on hand: one for plastic worms, one for spinnerbaits, one for plugs and spoons, one for jigs and tails, and so on.

Most generalists, on the other hand, operate out of one big box that holds a little of everything. Then there are those who do both — keep a main box around but use plastic "mini-boxes," carrying a single outing's worth of lures, for days they plan to travel light.

☞ Get good line and replace it often. A majority of Kansas fishing experts prefer clear monofilament line. Don't use line that is discolored or feels rough and stretched.

When adding new line to a spinning reel, make sure the line is coming off the package spool in the same direction it's going on your reel. If your reel winds counter-clockwise, the line should be unraveling counter-clockwise. This will prevent future tangles.

☞ Hooks are among the least expensive, yet most important, items you'll buy. Get the best and keep them sharp with a tackle-box file or sharpener. Sharp hooks are especially important when bass or striper fishing.

☞ Europeans have developed float fishing into an art form, especially when compared to the primitive state of American bobber fishing. The slender, sensitive floats used on streams in England shame our big red-and-white bubbles. If you can't find a respectable selection of floats for panfish, crappie and walleye fishing at your local sport shop, send for a catalog to Wazp Products, P.O. Box 837, Minden, Louisiana 71055.

☞ Weights come in all shapes and sizes and only experience will tell you what you need. Split-shot sinkers come in many sizes and are the most versatile for many types of inland, freshwater fishing. Bottom-walking weights are essential to some worm rigs used by walleye fishermen. Large, pyramid-shaped weights work best for surf-casing shad baits to striper country.

The ultimate weights for fishing in Kansas are downriggers, used for getting lures down to stripers in a deep lake such as Wilson. A downrigger weight is attached to a fishing line with a rubber band or small clamp. The weight is then lowered on its own winch to the desired depth, taking the lure down with it.

When a striper hits, it breaks the fishing line loose from the weight, allowing the angler to play the fish on an unencumbered line.

☞ Three-way swivels are necessary for setting up some multiple bait and lure rigs. Snap swivels can be convenient when changing lures frequently, and some lures work better on a swivel than when connected directly to the fishing line. Buy strong swivels and check the snaps before each use.

LURES

The quickest way to date a book would be to list the lures that were most popular in the year it was published. Instead, here's a list of major lures by category, along with tips about combinations that have proven consistently successful in Kansas.

Jigs. Among the most versatile of artificial lures, jigs come in a wide variety of shapes and sizes and are usually dressed up with either live bait or artificial trailers.

Small $\frac{1}{32}$, $\frac{1}{16}$ and $\frac{1}{8}$ ounce maribou jigs, with colorful tails that hang down the hook shank, can be very effective on panfish and crappie. While it sometimes helps to add a small minnow or worm, live baits aren't necessary. Favorite colors: white, chartreuse, orange, amber, black, yellow. It's usually best to use the smallest jig you can present effectively to the fish. This will

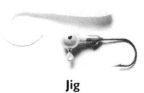

Jig

depend in part on the wind and waves. Be sure to tie the jig so that it "swims" like a suspended minnow, perpendicular to the line, and doesn't dangle limply downward.

Larger $\frac{1}{8}$ and $\frac{1}{4}$ ounce jigs are standard lures for crappie, white bass and walleye. Use maribou jigs with fur tails or attach plastic trailer tails on plain jig heads with bare hooks. Add minnows, as necessary, to lure strikes out of white bass and crappie; nightcrawlers work well on walleye. Dangle the jig directly into brushy cover hideouts and bounce it off the bottom along dropoffs.

"Jig-and-pig" combinations — a large jig hook with a pork-rind trailer — are exceptional spring largemouth bass lures. Cast up to brushy bank areas and slowly dance the lure back across the bottom. Blue jigs with green trailers seem to imitate bluegills well and can be deadly on Kansas lakes. Black and brown, coupled with orange, also works well.

Large jigs with plastic trailers work well when trolling deep water for stripers. White, blue and pink are good colors; they should feature plenty of sparkle.

Plastic jig dressings, which pull over the head of $\frac{1}{8}$ and $\frac{1}{4}$ ounce jigs, work well

on spotted bass and other stream fish. Sparkling blue, or black-and-chartreuse are favorite colors. Slowly bounce the jig across the bottom, as you would a plastic worm.

Jigs with spinning blades, such as Road Runners, are among the most popular and effective lures for catching white bass, especially during their shallow-water spring spawning runs.

Plastic worms. An essential largemouth bass lure, plastic worms come in more colors than you'll find in a 64-pack of Crayolas. On Kansas lakes and ponds, a touch of chartreuse never hurts. Black, green, hot pink, white and purple are other good colors. In clear streams, better have some blue.

Most all Kansans rig their worms "Texas style" so that it hangs straight down the hook from the line. Cast to likely bass cover, let the worm settle to the bottom, then flick your wrist to lift the worm and wriggle it forward several inches. Let it settle, then repeat. Add variety by moving the worm, from time to time, with several quick jerks, letting it fall back a little each time. Sometimes, you can even catch a bass by simply

Plastic worm

"swimming" a worm back, reeling it in as you would a spoon or a spinner.

Often, bass strike as the worm is drifting down and sometimes a hit can be hard to detect. If you sense a pause in the worm's fall, or if you see the line stop still or shift to the side, take up any slack and hold the bait steady. Should you detect any resistance at the other end, set the hook hard.

Plastic eels and lizards can provoke angry responses from spawning bass at a time when they aren't much interested in passing worm meals.

Spinnerbaits. These popular bass lures will also catch other predator species. They feature one or more rotating blades on an upper wire arm, a lead head, and a rubber skirt and hook on the lower arm.

Relatively weedless, they're easy to use — you can simply cast to cover and retrieve at varying speeds. Spinnerbaits work best when

Spinnerbait

dressed up with a plastic curly tail or a pork-rind trailer. White, black, blue, chartreuse and orange are the most common colors in spinnerbait combinations.

Spinnerbaits can be an excellent way to locate bass at the start of an outing. Cast spinnerbaits of various colors in a fan pattern and retrieve at several different speeds. Once a bass bites, you have an idea of where they're hiding, what they're eating and how fast they're moving. You can start developing a pattern for the day.

With blades of broad metal or plastic, spinnerbaits are transformed into buzzbaits, which clatter across the surface when retrieved at the proper speed. Like other surface lures, buzz baits work best on calm waters when the light is low and bass are rising to feed.

You can also let a spinnerbait settle to the bottom, then retrieve it slowly back like a jig-and-pig. Especially effective on smallmouth and spotted bass, this technique will fool largemouths hanging around a dropoff.

Small spinnerbaits with soft plastic bodies, such as Beetlespins, make very good bass, crappie and sunfish lures in Kansas streams and farm ponds. Orange, brown and green work well, as the lures likely resemble crayfish to the bass.

Floating minnows / crankbaits. Crafted of plastic or balsa wood, crankbaits generally imitate bait fish.

You can cast them toward bass structure, retrieve them along the edges of weedbeds, or troll them after walleye, white bass and stripers. Floating balsa minnows can be twitched across the surface when fish are rising to feed.

When trolling, remember that the dominant bait fish in Kansas reservoirs is the silver gizzard shad. Black and silver work well, with blue and white coming into play in deep water. Some of the most effective shad imitations include a built-in rattle.

Crankbait

To catch smallmouth and stream bass, bump crawdad colored imitations of brown, orange and green across rocky points, dropoffs and river bottoms.

Spinners and spoons. These are the oldest and most time-tested lures and every angler has his favorites. I rarely go anywhere without a French spinner, mainly because it was the first lure I ever threw that fooled a fish (a smallmouth bass).

However, spinners and spoons have a tendency to hang up quickly on stumps and snags, which litter the bottom of most Kansas

Spinner

reservoirs. Some farm ponds, community lakes and streams are free enough of obstacles for easy casting of spoons and spinners, but you'll have to find them on your own.

Weedless spoons can be decent lures in thick weedbeds.

Slab spoons, including Kastmasters, are among the most effective lures for catching white bass, stripers and walleye

Spoon

in deep reservoirs. Slab spoons, which imitate falling shad, are snapped off the bottom like jigs, then allowed to settle back down. Fish them directly over brush, humps, dropoffs and shad schools.

Topwaters. We humans are visual creatures and find nothing more exciting than seeing our prey take the bait.

Catching fish with surface lures is the most fun way to fish, and the most effective way when conditions are right.

Largemouth bass tend to hide in the shadows of logs, rocks and other cover during the bright light of

Topwater lure

day, as do most predator species. At dawn and dusk, however, and sometimes well into the night, the wolves of the water rise to feast on the insects and small animals swimming above.

Topwater baits imitate frogs, bugs and wounded minnows. Using light spinning gear, I prefer to cast smaller frog-colored topwater lures with propeller blades. Cast them out, let them sit for a moment, then flick them back across the water with short, quick jerks.

Poppers work the same way — dance them across the lake like frightened frogs.

Topwaters work best on still nights when the water is calm. Watch closely for signs of commotion, especially minnows leaping at the surface. It means predators are lurking nearby.

Cast past the commotion, then work your topwater bait back through it. Wait until you feel the strike before setting the hook. Often, anglers instinctively yank at the sight of a striking fish, and end up pulling the bait right out of its mouth.

Flyfishing for bass is becoming increasingly popular in Kansas and there are fly-tying clubs in the major cities. You can use anything from tiny dry flies to large imitation mice to catch bass on a fly rod. Two helpful books are: "Bass Flies" by Dick Steward, and L.L. Bean's "Flyfishing for Bass" by Dave Whitlock. Whitlock also has a video out on flyfishing for bass.

During a brief period each year, late in the summer, striped bass rise to feed on shad in the shallows, especially on Glen Elder Reservoir. Buzz baits and practically any other surface lure tossed in the maelstrom will be brutally attacked by the mighty school.

The excitement of surface fishing for stripers is matched only by the frustration of watching them straighten out hooks and snap off line. Manage to boat one of the beasts, however, and you'll have enjoyed perhaps the ultimate freshwater fishing experience.

GETTING AROUND

Sunlight dances along the waters of a gentle rapids on a branch of the Fall River. Oaks, hickorys, willows and bare-trunked sycamores rise high above. A woodpecker's drumming overpowers the music of cardinals and warblers. A quail whistles.

The cool water feels good as you enter the domain of stream bass. You test the bank with a few quick casts, then sit down in the float tube, lean against the back rest and kick your swim fins, cruising backward up the river at a comfortable pace.

You find a place where you can reach bottom and stand near the edge of a deep hole. You cast to a submerged log near the bank and let the worm settle down. As you jerk in the blue worm, the line jerks back.

You flick up the ultralight rod to set the hook and start a fight with a scrappy, 15-inch spotted bass.

The best things in life are rarely the most expensive and my favorite mode of transportation on Kansas streams, and even on some farm ponds and small lakes, is a float tube that cost less than $100.

It boasts side pockets for storing tackle, a back pocket big enough for a sandwich and two cans of pop, Velcro rod holders and an apron that serves as a workbench for tying on lures.

Most importantly, the tube enables me to slip among lily pads for pre-spawn bass

that can't be reached from big bass boats or from the tangled, brushy shore. In a tube, I can slowly, quietly cover every nook and cranny of a mud-bottomed stream without worrying about plunging into a hole and flooding my waders.

"Besides," says Wichitan Stan Muecke, an avid tube fisherman. "You feel like you're a lot more in tune with the fish when you're in the water with 'em. You're more in tune with the whole purpose of going outdoors."

Other handy, inexpensive vessels for streams, ponds and small lakes in Kansas include formed-plastic mini bass boats, john boats and canoes. Each has advantages and disadvantages

Mini bass boats provide good platforms for standing to cast. Powered by an electric trolling motor, a mini boat can cover a pond or watershed lake with ease and squeeze into tight spots where fish love to hide. They're not designed to handle rough water, however, and they don't maneuver well in strong winds, waves or currents. They are bulky and harder to transport than other small "cartopper" boats.

John boats also provide stable plat-

forms for casting in calm waters. Easy to maneuver on streams, they can be poled into weedy, marshy areas accessible only to flat-bottomed boats. They fit nicely on the roof of a car, or in the bed of a pickup, and they carry more passengers than a mini-boat or a canoe. But their flat hulls are no match for the rough, open waters of Kansas' windy reservoirs.

Canoes are the original North American watercraft and I believe every outdoorsman should own one. Nothing paddles as gracefully, nor handles streams as well. But standing in a canoe to cast can be tricky, especially for kids. And while experienced paddlers can steer a canoe through rough waters, the going can be slow, especially if you're trying to escape a sudden thunderstorm.

For the most part, Kansas is not nearly so violent a place as it was a century or so ago. You can travel anywhere in the state today without fear of being felled by a raging grassfire, a Kiowa arrow or a drunken gunslinger's bullet.

But there are a couple of things about the prairie that man has yet to tame: the wind and the weather.

In Kansas, a blue sky can become a roil-

Depending on the size of your fishing hole, you'll be best served by a bass boat, mini-deck platform, canoe or float tube.

ing black mass of wind, water and electricity in 15 minutes. If you're paying attention, and if your boat can motor, that should be enough time to get off of any reservoir in the state.

The best argument I've heard for acquiring a fishing boat with a semi-V hull and an outboard motor of at least 35 horsepower is that it could save your life.

A modern, semi-V hull features a bow that will slice through whitecaps, tapering back to a flat hull that provides a stable fishing platform. Modern outboard motors are generally more powerful and more reliable than their ancestors.

A new fiberglass bass boat with all the electronic gadgets can cost as much as a small house. If you're more concerned about function than style, however, you can find a practical new fishing machine for $5,000 or less.

The most boat I've seen for the buck was put together by Pratt fisherman Rob Manes. Scanning newspaper ads, Manes found an old ski boat, motor and trailer for $125.

"The trick is finding an aluminum one," Manes says. "Old fiberglass probably isn't going to treat you very well."

Manes had a 35-horse outboard rebuilt for $200. He ripped out the runabout's arched front deck, saving the flotation underneath. He glued the flotation to a new deck of half-inch plywood ($25), then bolted the deck to the hull with 90-degree brackets. Calk sealed the bolt holes, which were well above the water line.

Manes bought new steering cables ($10) and rigged them up the starboard side. He bolted a stern pedestal chair to the base of an old bench seat, and bolted a bow pedestal to the new plywood deck. The chairs cost $75.

Adding a new foot-controlled electric trolling motor ($275), a flasher depthfinder ($100), a liquid crystal fish locator ($175) and some indoor-outdoor carpeting to reduce the noise, the total cost came to just under $1,000.

Whenever he feels the need, Manes adds a $30 livewell to the package, using a cooler and a 12-volt pump.

BOATING IN KANSAS

It was after midnight late one summer when the fishermen quit drifting for channel catfish on El Dorado Reservoir.

Heading for shore, they glimpsed a

RULES OF THE ROAD

☞ When two vessels approach head on, each keeps to the starboard (right). When passing a vehicle going in the same direction, keep well clear of it and watch your wake.

☞ When two vessels' paths are crossing, the one on the port (left) must yield right of way.

☞ Any vessel propelled by machinery must be kept clear of any vessel under sail or propelled by oars.

A rhyme worth remembering:
Here lies the body of Thomas
    Day;
He died asserting his right of way,
Now Tom was right as he
    sailed along,
But he's just as dead as if he
    were wrong!

light flickering weakly in the distance. At first, they thought it was the light of another fishing boat, flashing in and out of sight as it wound through the trees. But when the light didn't appear to move after several minutes, they decided to check it out.

An entire family, including small children, had been marooned by a dead motor. Lost and frightened, they had blinked the flashlight for hours, they said, but nobody had noticed. The fishermen who towed them in turned out to be the last boaters on the lake that night.

The family was lucky — the weather had stayed calm and warm until somebody had found them. They learned a valuable lesson about the need to keep distress signals on their boat.

Practical nighttime distress signals include flare guns, high-intensity white lights which flash every second, and distress flashlights which automatically signal SOS with three short blinks, followed by three long flashes, followed by three short blinks.

Daytime distress symbols include orange smoke signals or a distress flag, at least 3 feet by 3 feet, with a black square and ball on an orange background. Fly the flag from a mast or wave it on a paddle.

All boats, including canoes and kayaks, must have a Coast Guard approved lifejacket or throwable flotation device for each person on board.

More than 80 percent of the people who die in boating accidents drown, according to Coast Guard statistics, and most were not wearing a personal flotation device. The Coast Guard grades personal flotation devices in four major classes.

Type I lifejackets have the greatest buoyancy and are designed to turn an unconscious person from face down in the water to vertical and slightly backward.

Type II lifejackets are also designed to hold a person vertical and slightly backward, but the turning action isn't as great as with Type I. Type II jackets are easier to wear than Type I and are recommended for children.

Type III devices are designed so wearers can put themselves in a safe position and hold it without effort.

Type IV devices are designed to be thrown to a person in the water so they can hang on until rescued.

All sailboats and vessels propelled by machinery must be registered and numbered by the state. Applications are available from marine dealers, county clerks and the Kansas Department of Wildlife and Parks, Permit Division, Route 2, Box 54A, Pratt, Kansas 67124. Registration costs $9 for three years. A 30-day permit costs $2.50.

Small boats must have a lantern or flashlight handy to avoid collisions. Larger boats need running lights. Motorboats (including sailboats with motors) need fire extinguishers on board. Types of lights, extinguishers and flotation required vary according to boat size. Check with the Coast Guard or Wildlife and Parks for details about your boat.

No one under 12 can operate a motorboat in Kansas unless supervised by someone over 17. You many not operate a boat, surfboard, waterskis or similar devices while under the influences of drugs or alcohol. You must keep out of areas protected by buoys and your wake cannot endanger others.

ACCESSORIES

Depth finders have so changed the world of sport fishing in recent years that they might not qualify as accessories anymore. For many boat fishermen, depth finders are no less important than a motor or a pair of oars.

There are three major types of depth finders, or fish locators: the flasher, the paper recorder and the liquid crystal display monitor.

All three types send sonar signals below the boat, then measure how long it takes for the echoes to bounce back.

Flashers are inexpensive yet highly informative to trained eyes. An experienced angler can zip across a lake at full throttle, keeping one eye on the flasher for signs of structural diversity.

In older reservoirs, where silt has leveled the highs and lows of the lake bottom, even slight variations, such as a channel three feet deep, act as fish magnets., Variations in the lake bottom show up clearly on flashers, especially when used in conjunction with a topographic map.

Schools of gizzard shad — the primary forage of reservoir gamefish — often appear as pillar columns, or steep peaks, or clouds on depth finders. Once you've found shad, you will often find stripers, whites, walleye and crappie feeding on them.

Another way to locate fish is to use a depthfinder in conjunction with trolling or drifting. When you get a hit while trolling, toss out a marker buoy. Once the fish is landed, return to the area marked by the buoy and study it with your depthfinder, searching for any structure that might have attracted a fish to that spot. If you find a dropoff, a brushpile or a hump, park directly over it and see if other fish are lurking there.

Later, you can search for similar structures elsewhere on the lake.

Paper chart recorders provide by far the most detailed and accurate information about what lies below your boat. Fish appear as boomerang marks on the paper charts, which are especially good at finding the larger species, such as stripers.

A gray line on the chart tells experienced anglers whether the surface below is soft or firm — an important point when, say, you're trying to find an old gravel railroad bed often traveled by walleye.

Liquid crystal displays are rapidly growing in popularity. They present fairly detailed information in an easy-to-read video format. The detail provided by liquid crystal units has improved sharply in recent years and they may one day provide as clear a picture of the lake as paper charts now do.

Liquid crystal units vary widely in price and quality. Get advice from experienced anglers about which type of depth finder would best suit your particular needs.

Trolling motors have also done a great deal to increase the ease and versatility of boat fishing. Anglers rarely need anchors anymore, now that they can maneuver a boat exactly where they want it, and keep it there, with just a few taps on a pedal.

When choosing a trolling motor, don't look merely at price — consider your boat's size as well. Every 200 pounds of weight requires five pounds of thrust. A bass boat weighing in at 1,000 pounds (including motor, batteries, gear, fuel, livewell water and passengers) will require at least 25 pounds of thrust.

Obviously, a 24-volt trolling motor

provides much more power than a 12-volt motor. Electric motors also are better at pulling boats than pushing them; most fishermen mount trolling motors near the bow.

Be sure to get the proper shaft length on your motor — they vary from 30 to 42 inches long. A john boat, for instance, requires a much shorter staff than a semi-V hull.

Other important accessory items include:

☞ A sharp filet knife. If you'll be catching a large number of small fish, such as crappie or white bass, you might consider buying an electric filet knife that hooks up to a 12-volt trolling motor battery.

☞ A pocket knife or nail clippers, for snipping line, and so on. Many anglers keep a clippers tied to a string that hangs from their necks.

☞ A pliers. The best way to release fish unharmed is to grab the hook shank with a pliers and shake it. Pliers also come in handy to fix and fine-tune lures, swivels and other equipment.

☞ Sunscreen and sunglasses that protect against ultraviolet rays.

☞ A rain suit or parka. You never know when you'll need it.

☞ Maps showing key structure in the water you'll be fishing.

☞ A first aid kit.

☞ A lake thermometer.

☞ A color gauge that measures water quality and suggests lure color choices.

☞ A stringer, livewell, or cooler, for taking fish home.

BOAT MAINTENANCE

Every spring, Kansas marine mechanics are faced with cracked engine blocks, plugged carburetors and myriad other engine problems that could have been prevented with proper off-season maintenance.

"About 90% of the people do not properly winterize in the fall. It's totally unbelievable," according to Brent Hopkins, owner of Fish and Ski Marine in Wichita.

Half of all boat owners do no winterizing whatever, said Danny Carter, shop foreman at Wichita's L&M Marine.

Owners of boats with inboard/outboard engines have the most to fear from winter. While an outboard motor will drain itself if left upright, an inboard/outboard must have stops pulled in several places to get water out of the engine block, exhaust manifolds, exhaust elbows and power steering cooler. If water in these compartments isn't drained and replaced with anti-freeze, it could freeze and expand, causing expensive motor damage.

Simply pulling the stop-cocks isn't always enough to fully drain the motor. Sand and rust particles can plug drain holes. "The guy thinks he's drained his block, then you poke a screwdriver up there and all this water flows out," Hopkins said.

To winterize an inboard/outboard, you should:

☞ Add gasoline stabilizer to the fuel and fill the gas tank to the brim. Run the engine in water and check its overall performance. Check especially that it is not running hot, indicating a possible water pump problem. Check the engine's compression and spark.

☞ Cut the fuel supply to the motor and continue running until all the fuel in the engine is expended. When gas remains with oil in carburetors, the mixture can form a shellac that plugs carburetor jets. Remove the spark plugs and air breather. Spray storage oil down the throat of the carburetor until it runs out the spark plug holes. Replace the plugs.

☞ Drain all water in the engine and replace with antifreeze. Hopkins cautions people to use a biodegradable antifreeze, as the mixture will be flushed into a lake the next time the boat is operated.

☞ Drain oil in the upper and lower drive units by removing flathead drain screws. Never remove Allen or Phillips screws. Water can get into the drive unit oil, causing it to freeze if not replaced with fresh oil. Refill the drive unit from the bottom hole until it comes out the top (vent) hole.

☞ Charge the battery. A charged battery is less likely to freeze.

☞ Check all hoses, belts and cables.

☞ Apply grease at all zerks.

☞ Apply grease to trailer wheel bearings. Check the lug nuts and tire pressure.

☞ Manufacturers generally recommend that inboard/outboard owners also replace the engine oil and filter, and have the water pump checked before winter. Checking and repacking the trailer wheel bearings is a good idea.

Fewer problems arise with outboard motors in cold weather, but winterizing still provides strong preventive medicine for many common engine problems.

Each fall, an outboard owner should:

☞ Add stabilizer to fuel and fill the tank. Run the motor in water and check overall operation. If the water pump is working properly, the outboard's cylinder head should feel lukewarm or cool. Check engine compression and spark.

☞ Cut the fuel supply and run the motor until all gas is expended. Remove spark plugs and spray storage oil down the throat of each carburetor until it comes out the corresponding spark plug hole. Replace the plugs.

☞ Store the motor upright until it has drained completely.

☞ Drain oil in the lower unit by removing flathead drain screws. Refill from bottom hole to top.

☞ Remove the propeller and make sure the shaft is clear of fishing line. Monofilament can cut through shaft seals, causing the lower unit to lose oil and gain water. Grease the shaft before replacing the prop. Get the prop repaired during the winter if necessary.

☞ Charge the battery.

☞ Apply grease at motor and trailer zerks.

Dealers in the area will perform these services for a set fee. It is wise to bring your boat to dealers authorized to work on your model, so you don't wind up, like a friend of mine once did, with a jury-rigged Mercury throttle mechanism on an Evinrude motor.

With proper winterization and maybe a second battery charge, a boat owner will be able to head straight to his favorite lake on the first warm day of spring.

Section Two

The Quarry

ARE SOME FISH SPECIES smarter and more difficult to catch than others? Don't ask a fisherman. ⚡ There's an old saying that you can always tell when a fisherman is lying. If his mouth is moving, he's lying. ⚡ That saying is true. ⚡ Not only are fishermen liars, but they are prejudiced.

Each harbor favorite species, even those who claim, "I fish for whatever's biting. I don't care what it is."

Elden Bailey claims that. Bailey, who produces a Lawrence radio program on fishing, has twice shared the Kansas state walleye fishing championship with long-time partner Gary Miller. Bailey also is a charter member of the Kansas Walleye Association.

Funny, for a guy who says he doesn't play favorites, but Bailey has never belonged to a bass fishing association. He's never won, or even entered, a crappie tournament.

So tell us what you really think, Elden.

"You could toss out a ski rope that has an old tennis shoe with a treble hook on it, and sooner or later you'd catch a bass," he says, with a little prodding. "I've fished for every species in this part of the country and walleye's the toughest, year-in, year-out."

Bruce Coate also says he fishes for whatever's hot, never mind the color. And as Kansas' only fulltime fishing guide, he does fish for a variety of species on Wilson Lake. Yet Coate toured the nation for several years, enjoying great success in striper tournaments from South Carolina

to Colorado. I've never heard him tell old stories about his days on the bass or walleye tournament circuits.

So tell us what you really think, Bruce.

"I think the bass is an awful dumb fish myself," Coate says, needing no more spark than it took to launch Bailey. "The walleye can be a pretty smart fish — but not near as smart as a striper."

I've had the great pleasure of fishing for largemouth bass with friendly Kurt Geis, of Wichita, who competes regularly in regional bass tournaments. Geis often has said to me: "If the bass aren't biting, maybe we'll just go after crappie or something."

He never has said, "If the crappie aren't biting, maybe we'll just go after bass." Nor have I ever heard him refer to a fellow member of the Kansas Bassmasters as a "perch jerker."

So tell us what you really think, Kurt.

"I think that most of us bass fishermen that refer to perch jerkers are talking about the guys who will drown a minnow fishing for anything that will bite," he says. "It's not meant in a derogatory sense."

Of course not. Who would dream that "perch jerker" was anything other than a complimentary term?

As you can see, fishermen are not supe-

HANDLING A TROPHY

Whether you catch a 30-pound striper, a 12-pound walleye or a 10-pound largemouth, take closeup color photographs of the fish immediately after catching it if you want a natural looking mount.

A skilled taxidermist will use the photo as a guide for painting the trophy. After taking the pictures, wrap the fish in wet towels or newspaper and keep it in a cool spot. Once you get home, lay the fish on a board and surround it with several tight layers of plastic wrap, then seal it in a plastic garbage bag and freeze it until you can bring it to a taxidermist.

Try to find a taxidermist who has experience mounting game fish and is knowledgeable about the species you are bringing him. Ask for references. The best preservers of deer heads aren't necessarily the best at duplicating the

poses and colors of trophy fish, although many taxidermists are highly skilled with both fish and game.

rior to other human beings in every way. They share a flaw universal to their species. To add to their entertainment, they tend to associate in groups of people who share similar tastes. And nothing seems more entertaining to one group of people than to ridicule the members of another group.

As a result, walleye fishermen poke fun at bass anglers who tell jokes about panfish enthusiasts. Everyone belittles catfishermen — especially fly fishermen, who belittle everyone.

Aiming to increase angling pleasure, marine biologists have developed new ammunition for these cliques of fishermen to hurl at one another. Recent research indicates that gamefish species do, in fact, possess different capacities for learning. Some species appear to catch on very quickly that certain threatening objects — such as fishing lures — should be avoided. Other species, to put it politely, catch on less quickly.

"They're dumb," said Richard Frie, a natural resources professor at the University of Wisconsin-Stevens Point.

Researchers assume that "smart" species are more challenging to catch with consistency.

If they're correct, which of the above fisherman gets to keep his bragging rights, judging solely from intelligence test results?

Coate — the striper man. Striped bass consistently rate among the fastest learners in the fish kingdom, Frie said.

Largemouth bass, on the other hand, consistently rank near the bottom of the class in intelligence tests, behind bullhead, but ahead of the supremely stupid northern pike.

Walleye and channel catfish tend to grade as "C" students.

Bass eventually will learn not to strike lures that smack back, Frie said. It just takes them a little longer.

STATE RECORDS

To be eligible for a state record, a legally taken trophy fish must be weighed on a certified scale in front of witnesses. No-body may have helped the angler hook, play or land the fish.

SPECIES	WEIGHT(LBS)	PLACE/YEAR	ANGLER
Largemouth	11.75	Farm Pond, 1977	Kenneth Bingham
Smallmouth	5.56	Wilson Res., 1988	Rick O'Bannon
Spotted	4.44	Marion Co. Lake, 1977	Clarence McCarter
Striper	43.50	Wilson Res., 1988	Chester Nily
White bass	5.25	Toronto Res., 1966	Henry Baker
Bluegill	2.31	Farm Pond, 1962	Robert Jeffries
Blue catfish	82.00	Kansas River, 1988	Preston Stubbs, Jr.
Flathead cat	87.50	Pomona Res., 1990	Jerry Griffin
Channel cat	33.75	Kansas River, 1980	Larry Wright
Black crappie	4.63	Woodson St. Lake, 1957	Hazel Fey
White crappie	4.02	Farm Pond, 1964	Frank Miller
Walleye	13.06	Rocky Ford, 1972	David Watson
Wiper	18.94	Milford Res., 1990	Lone Bounsombath
Northern	24.75	Council Grove Res., 1971	H.A. Bowman
Green sunfish	2.37	Farm Pond, 1982	Fae Vaupel
Redear sun	1.46	Mined Lands, 1983	Pat Whetzell

"Studies show that largemouth bass and other fish are capable of learning to avoid baits," he said. "They can remember a bad experience for up to an entire season."

It's unlikely that anything remains in a bass' brain for longer than one fishing season, Frie added.

When forced to face the facts of modern science, Geis weakened momentarily and admitted there were sunken logs with greater mental powers than a young largemouth.

"Once I caught the same 10-inch fish 12 times in a row before he finally figured out that the plastic worm bit back," Geis said. "An 8 to 10 inch bass is really dumb, but their level of learning would have to improve as they get more mature."

Precisely, said Frie, who strongly supports catch-and-release fishing for bass. Populations of aggressive bass can be rapidly depleted from heavily fished waters, he says, unless the slow-learning fish are allowed to try, try again.

Anyone familiar with the fate of El Dorado Reservoir knows what Frie means. Anglers could reel 100 bass out of El Dorado's newly flooded timber in just a couple of hours during the spring and summer of 1984. By 1986, professional bass fishermen with top-notch equipment often had to churn El Dorado's waters from dawn until dusk to uncover a couple of keepers.

"Releasing your catch helps keep those aggressive, fast growing and 'less smart' fish in the water for us to catch again," Frie said. "Maybe those fish will spawn and produce offspring with a similar vulnerability to angling."

In other words, Frie suggested, fishermen prefer stupid fish, because they are easier to catch.

Wichita marine dealer Brent Hopkins makes no bones about why he prefers channel catfish over Kansas' other sporting species, including the bass his father raised him on. "With channel catfish, you get a limit on all but the real bad days," he said. "It's easier to catch more of them. They put up as hard a fight, or harder. It's something the family can enjoy — my 4-year-old can catch them."

Fish intelligence levels may also help explain why so few Kansas fishermen hunt the common carp. Carp consistently rank among the smartest of fish, along with the equally unpopular bigmouth buffalo, Frie said.

He cautioned that fish aptitude tests may contain hidden social biases that favor cautious species, such as carp, while discriminating against bass, pike and other hooligans.

"Bass seem dumb," Frie said. "Well, maybe a bass knows better, but because it's such an aggressive fish, it just has to hit that lure anyway."

Fish IQ tests also fail to account for differing levels of intelligence within species, argued Geis.

"I know for a fact that keeper-sized bass are the smartest fish of all when you're in a tournament," he said.

Few anglers who have competed in a bass tournament will argue with that.

About the only thing that fish intelligence tests confirm for sure is that par-

MASTER ANGLERS

If you lawfully catch a fish of exceptional size, the Department of Wildlife and Parks will issue you a Master Angler Award. Applications appear on fishing regulations brochures at all license outlets. Minimum weights eligible for the most popular species are:

Largemouth bass	7 pounds
Smallmouth bass	3 pounds
Spotted bass	2 pounds
Striped bass	15 pounds
White bass	3 pounds
Walleye	6 pounds
Bluegill	1 pound
Channel catfish	15 pounds
Flathead catfish	35 pounds*
Crappie	3 pounds
Green sunfish	1 pound

*(50 pounds on setline)

ticular fishermen are attracted to particular methods of fishing for particular types of fish.

Whether your tastes run toward gracefully drifting dry flies on a wooded stream, or casting toward a brushpile where an explosive largemouth lurks, or checking setlines for underwater monsters in the darkness of a new moon at midnight, Kansas has a fish for you.

T HREE SPECIES OF BLACK BASS live in Kansas: the largemouth, smallmouth and spotted or "Kentucky" bass. All three are really oversized sunfish with nasty dispositions — more closely related to bluegill than to white bass, striped bass or other members of the sea bass family.

LARGEMOUTH

Of Kansas' black bass species, the largemouth draws by far the most attention, for several reasons.

First, largemouth lurk in rivers, ponds, lakes and reservoirs throughout the state. In contrast, spotted bass stick mostly to streams in the eastern third of the state, while smallmouth have an unfortunate preference for clear, deep waters with rocky shores — a rare combination in Kansas.

Second, largemouth are the heavyweights of the black bass world, which adds to their prestige, though smallmouth and spotted bass probably pack more punch per pound. The state record spotted bass weighed 4.44 pounds, smallmouth weighed 5.56 and largemouth weighed 11.75. The world record spotted weighed 8.94 pounds, smallmouth weighed 11.94 and largemouth weighed 22.25.

Nothing, however, has more to do with the popularity of largemouth bass fishing in Kansas today than the nationwide interest stirred up by big-money bass tournaments. In less than 20 years, they have transformed an idle pastime into a highly competitive sport. A huge marine and tackle industry has developed hand-in-hand with tournament bass fishing.

While smallmouth and spotted bass can also be weighed in at the tournaments, it's hard to catch them as efficiently, pound-for-pound. Tournament fishermen, working on a strict time deadline, prize efficiency.

Pick up a national outdoor sports magazine in winter, spring or summer and you're likely to find several feature stories and tips on catching largemouth bass. At least half-a-dozen national publications cater to nothing but bass fishermen, including "Bassmaster," which George Bush listed as his favorite magazine during the 1988 presidential campaign.

Like the rest of us outdoor magazine buffs, the President likely is mailed seasonal catalogs from Bass Pro Shops, Cabela's and other sporting goods retailers that run heavy on largemouth bass fishing equipment. Instructional books and videos about largemouth bass fishing abound. Run through the TV channels on any Saturday or Sunday afternoon and you're bound to find a program about largemouth bass fishing. Stop by the local sport, boat and travel show and you can spend hours strolling by the new bass boat rigs; the bass rods, reels and lures; the bass fishing accessories; and the giant aquariums stocked with hungry bass for casting demonstrations by professional largemouth bass fishermen.

There was a time, not so long ago, when knowledge about bass and other gamefish was passed down — often reluctantly — from weathered veterans to persistent youngsters. Classes were held on a dock or in a row boat.

Today, folks pack into theaters, at $3 a head, to hear the advice of a famous bass pro making the rounds on the off-season seminar circuit. You practically have to shield your eyes when a star like Jimmy Houston strides into the stagelights, his yellow sweat suit matching his mop of blond hair, a gold watch on one wrist, gold bracelet on the other.

"I can probably tell y'all everything I know about bass fishin' in two hours," Houston begins.

He's lying of course, which further endears him to the crowd, because it shows that, beneath all the glitz beats the heart of a true fisherman.

The basics of largemouth bass fishing are probably simple enough to be taught in two hours. But it's the particulars that separate Anglers of the Year from struggling tour pros, and struggling tour pros from regional heroes, and regional heroes from club champs, and club champs from experienced leisure fishermen, and experienced leisure fishermen from beginners. These particulars take longer to learn because experience remains the best teacher.

Randy Stovall, who won a couple dozen regional bass tournaments in the 1980s, once tried to describe for me how light the fish had been hitting on a fine spring morning. "I tossed a jig into the bush," he said. "It just seemed to stop sooner than it should. I set the hook. The fish weighed a little over six pounds."

Most anglers would have missed that "strike" no matter how much they had read

Largemouth Bass

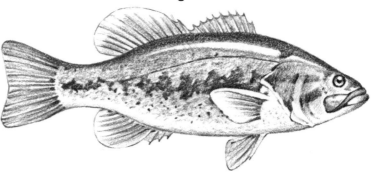

or watched about bass fishing. Practice and experience are necessary to hone your predatory instincts to where you can sense when a fish is merely sniffing your lure.

It took time for Stovall to develop his fishing sense. Like everyone else, he caught his first bass almost by accident. He was already 16 years old.

"Dad was blind," he said. The only way he could do any activity with my brother Bruce and I was to fish. Every Saturday and Sunday night, we'd go down on the Central Street Bridge (in Wichita). Our whole weekend was based on fishing."

They fished for carp and catfish in the Arkansas River. When oldest son Randy turned 16 and got a driver's license, his father bought a boat. Randy drove the family to Table Rock Lake in Missouri where, casting randomly, he caught a 7½ pound largemouth.

"I was hooked," he said.

There was a problem, however.

"Big bodies of water bothered me," he said. I could go to an area and catch a fish, but I didn't know why and I didn't know how to catch another one."

Stovall read everything he could find about largemouth bass hideouts and habits — his favorite book is Roland Martin's

Bass Fishing Secrets. He joined one of Wichita's six or seven bass fishing clubs and fished in the monthly club tournaments.

An apprenticeship of six years followed before he finally had learned enough to win his first cash bass tournament. The competition in bass tournaments these days is tough.

That can make bass fishing more difficult for everyone, including those who don't compete on any level. Competitive bass anglers put intense pressure on reservoir largemouth populations. While tournament fishermen release most everything they catch, a bass becomes harder to trick the more often it has been hooked.

On the other hand, tournament fishermen have greatly increased the available knowledge about bass habits and habitats while developing sophisticated ways to find and catch the fish. Here are a few things worth remembering about largemouth bass:

☞ They hear better than they see, picking up sound vibrations along their lateral line. The muddier the water, the more they rely on hearing.

☞ They become fairly blind in bright light — their pupils can't adjust to take in more or less light as ours do, and they have no eyelids for "squinting." When the sun is high and bright, they head for the shade of stumps, logs, docks, weedbeds, lilypads, submerged trees or deep water. Concentrate on structure, weedbeds and dropoffs in the middle of the day.

☞ During periods of dim light — dawn, dusk and nighttime — bass can see better near the surface and often rise to feed on minnows, insects, frogs and the like. An angler should then shift focus from structure fishing to surface baits, especially when the water is calm.

☞ Bass often hunt in shallow water on cloudy, windy days. Waves muddy the bottom, screening out sunlight. Wave action also oxygenates the water and pushes baitfish toward the shallows. You'll enjoy better success on a shore buffeted by wind and waves than on a calm, lee shore.

☞ Bass can see colors. As night descends, bass will sometimes suddenly ignore a lure they found irresistible moments earlier. This may be because the changing light has caused the lure to look different or become less visible. Switching colors often reignites the action.

☞ In spring and fall, when water temperatures vary most around a lake, you can generally find bass seeking water in the high 60s or low 70s. Bass begin to spawn once the surface temperature reaches 67 or 68 degrees (late March, early April in Kansas). Males build the nests in very shallow water and guard them as the larger females "stage" nearby, usually in four to seven feet of water. If you are catching 15-inch fish against the bank, females of 20 or more inches may be lurking on the other side of the boat.

Males continue guarding the nests for a week or so after the female has dropped her 2,000 to 20,000 eggs. Once the spawning is complete, bass head to deeper water.

With these facts in mind as you size up a reservoir, try to determine where the bass will not be before you start fishing. This generally eliminates at least three-fourths of the lake, depending on the season, so you can concentrate your efforts on finding fish in the much smaller body of water that remains.

In early spring, for example, the cold-blooded largemouth seeks the warmest spots of the reservoir and heats up for mating season. The relatively shallow water of incoming streams warms up sooner than the deep lower portion of a reservoir near the dam.

Concentrate on the pathways bass are likely to follow into warm water. With the aid of a map and/or a depthfinder, find where old creek and river channels approach points in the shallow end of the lake.

In the heat of an early spring day, bass often will rise from a channel up the hill of a point to forage for an hour or more. Lilting a spinnerbait slowly against the bottom — pulling the rod tip back in jerks and then reeling in the slack — sometimes attracts a strike on the lure's fall. Slowly retrieved crankbaits also work well.

Check out old road beds or fencerows that offer structural shade and ambush cover for bass on their way to shallow water. Don't stray too far from stream channels, which bass use as highways to spawning water.

"I start as far as a mile from where it (the channel) becomes a creek, fishing every area where the channel comes close to the bank," Stovall says. "I like to follow creeks, feeders, depressions up to where there's no water, then work back out to find where the fish have stopped."

Learn as much as you can from the first catch of the day. What kind of structure were you fishing near? How fast were you retrieving the lure? How deep was the water? What was the surface temperature?

Whatever forces attracted the bass to that place will be working on others of his stripe. Find similar spots, with help from your map, and you'll probably find more bass as well.

Accurate casting is essential to bass fishing, especially when fish are in shallow water and can be easily spooked by a clumsy presentation. Many bass fishermen spend hours in the backyard, casting practice plugs into buckets, perfecting their techniques like a golfer practices putts and chip shots. An underhand flip cast is especially useful for delicately landing spinnerbaits in shallow water against a bank. Besides enabling you to land a lure like a leaf on the water, the underhand cast can slip spinners and jigs under overhanging branches.

In Kansas, the most popular springtime bass lures are spinnerbaits and jig-and-

BLACK BASS CONVERSION TABLE

Based on average weight for bass of various lengths.

INCHES	POUNDS	INCHES	POUNDS
12	.84	18	3.37
12¼	.90	18¼	3.54
12½	.96	18½	3.71
12¾	1.03	18¾	3.88
13	1.10	19	4.06
13¼	1.18	19¼	4.25
13½	1.25	19½	4.44
13¾	1.34	19¾	4.64
14	1.42	20	4.84
14¼	1.51	20¼	5.06
14½	1.60	20½	5.27
14¾	1.70	20¾	5.50
15	1.80	21	5.73
15¼	1.91	21¼	5.97
15½	2.02	21½	6.21
15¾	2.13	21¾	6.48
16	2.25	22	6.72
16¼	2.37	22¼	6.99
16½	2.50	22½	7.26
16¾	2.63	22¾	7.54
17	2.77	23	7.83
17¼	2.92	23¼	8.12
17½	3.06	23½	8.43
17¾	3.22	23¾	8.74
24 and above		Weigh it!	

pigs — heavy jigs with rubber skirts and pork-rind trailers. Artificial lures are more efficient than live bait on a predator like the largemouth, which is triggered more by sight and sound than by smell. You can fish more bass cover with far greater speed by casting artificial baits. You'll also hook fish in the lip, for an easy live release, rather than in the stomach.

Largemouth prefer to spawn on gently sloping banks covered with fine gravel, if you can find such spots.

After spawn, they will usually be found around structure — the more of it the

better. A log at the edge of a dropoff, with one end in three feet of water, the other in 15 feet, is excellent, especially if the drop-off occurs where a point nears a river channel. Add a switchback loop in the channel and the area is even more likely to hold largemouth and other gamefish.

As summer progresses, remember the

When bass strike consistently in a given area, pay attention to details such as water depth and lure retrieval.

temperature range preferred by bass and ignore shallow spawning areas where the water has become too warm. Bass may still work the shallows for food, but they will rise from cooler water in spurts, then retreat to a more comfortable depth.

Favorite summer lures for working around structure include spinnerbaits, plastic worms and rubber crawdad imitations, plus crankbaits that resemble gizzard shad, minnows or crayfish. When bass are hiding in the shade of thick cover, such as lilypads or the branches of a submerged tree, try lowering a plastic worm or crayfish, rigged Texas-style, then simply shake it to trigger a response.

If you see minnows trying to jump out of the lake, or other signs of surface activity, cast a buzz bait past the commotion, then reel back through it. Or twitch a floating topwater lure, a floating balsa minnow, an imitation frog. Bass sometimes attack topwater lures with brutal force — set the hook when you feel the fish, not when you see it, or you might yank it away a second too soon.

Flyfishing can be fantastic on bass in summertime, especially on farm ponds and streams. Cast mice and bassbugs to holes and pockets in the weeds and wait for the splash. Damselflies and dragonfly nymphs work well on Kansas bass. You'll need 8-weight flyline, a strong shock tippet and a stiff rod for setting the hook.

Productive farm ponds offer the best bass fishing in Kansas. Spring-fed ponds tend to be good year after year if they aren't overfished. Most state fishing lakes and community lakes hold at least fair numbers of largemouth. In any given year, a few will offer excellent action thanks to several years of good production and low pressure, or to a recent state rehabilitation project. You'll have to figure out for yourself which ones are hot this year. A brief conversation with the Wildlife and Parks regional fisheries biologist will start you in the right direction.

Reservoirs that tend to hold the highest largemouth bass populations, year after year, include Big Hill, Hillsdale, El Dorado, Glen Elder, Wilson and Clinton.

BASS CLUBS

Thanks to the interest stirred up by tournament fishing, bass clubs have sprung up all across Kansas. At last count, there were seven bass clubs in Wichita alone.

Most experts strongly recommend clubs to anglers who have a serious desire to learn more about bass fishing.

Back in 1978, Leroy Anderson and six friends formed a small fishing club in Wichita. At the time, they did most of their fishing out of john boats on Flint Hills ponds, hence the name Flint Hills Bass Club.

"Everything we read said that the best way to learn more about bass fishing was to belong to a club," Anderson said. "None of the existing clubs fit our requirements."

Actually, Anderson and friends didn't feel they met the existing clubs' requirements. Their boats were small, their equipment meager.

A decade later, all that had changed. Flint Hills Bass Club — the largest group in the Kansas Bass Federation — won its second-straight intra-city tournament between Wichita bass fishing associations.

"I noticed at our last tournament that the smallest motor was a 115-horse," Anderson said. "In the early days that would have been by far the biggest motor there was."

Bass clubs generally hold a tournament every month for members during the warm half of the year. Contests run from about 6 a.m. to 4 p.m., with each member contributing an entry fee of $15 to $25 into a kitty that is later returned

SMALLMOUTH

Often associated with cold, clear northern waters, smallmouth bass now range south to Texas and west to California. No mat-

Most bass clubs hold monthly tournaments for members during the warm half of the year.

get involved from time to time in affairs of community and state.

Entry fees for the Wichita intra-city tournament, for example, are donated to the charity of the winning club's choice. Thanks in large part to strong support from bass clubs, a new state fish hatchery was built below Milford Reservoir in the early 1980s. Several bass clubs have participated in litter-cleanup campaigns around state reservoirs.

Bass clubs have had by far their biggest social impact in the successful promotion of catch-and-release bass fishing, which was unheard of 20 years ago but is widely practiced today.

In club tournaments, fish over 12 inches are measured in quarter-inch increments with a standard metal "board" carried in each boat. After being measured, the fish are immediately returned to the water. Weights are calculated with the aid of a table that converts inches into pounds. An angler's top five fish are added up to figure his total score.

"We use the honor system," Anderson said. "We've never had a problem with it, and I don't expect that we ever will."

The positive impact of catch-and-release is obvious at a heavily fished reservoir, such as El Dorado, where biologist Ron Marteney calculated that fishermen caught some 43,500 largemouth in one year alone — 88 percent of the lake's total estimated bass population.

Information about bass clubs in any particular area is easy to come by at bait shops, outdoor sports stores, marinas and boat dealers.

in prizes. Usually, members are teamed up with a different partner for each tournament to better spread the fishing knowledge around.

"One thing about competitive fishing — it makes you a better manager of your time," Anderson said.

Competitive club fishermen drive fast, paying $12,000 or more for a boat and motor that zips them from one likely hot spot to the next with a minimum of down time. The less time in transit, the more time spent with a lure in the water.

Anderson, for example, drives an 18-foot fiberglass boat that is mostly fishing deck. Powered by a 150-horse outboard, it cruises over 60 miles per hour.

Competitive fishermen keep several poles within easy reach, each rigged with a different jig or spinnerbait. When a lure becomes hot, however, the extra rods are ignored.

Though their primary purpose is for recreation and education, bass clubs also

ter where they live, they prefer water of 65 degrees or less when they can find it.

In Kansas, where the hot summers warm up shallow waters beyond the

smallmouth comfort zone, it takes to the deep, rarely feeding at the surface like its big-mouthed cousin.

Once reeled to the surface, however, a

smallmouth tends to put on a furious aerial display — flipping, thrashing and leaping in resistance.

Smallmouth Bass

Restless predators, smallmouth bass wander farther from home territory than largemouth do. Still, they generally are found around certain types of structure, including:

☞ Rocky points and dropoffs — the steeper the better

☞ Rip-rap around dams

☞ Steep-rising humps, particularly in the deep portion of a reservoir, near the dam

☞ The walls of river channels, especially along the deep outside bends

☞ Submerged rock ledges, walls and boulders

The more of these features a spot holds, of course, the more time smallmouth will spend there.

Smallmouth feed primarily on minnows, shad and crayfish, with the latter ranking as their favorite food. Minnows and crayfish make excellent live baits for smallmouth, which also smash properly presented spoons, spinnerbaits and deep-running crankbaits.

Anything resembling a crawdad can draw a hit, especially if the lure is worked carefully across rocky structure on the bottom. A spinnerbait, rigged with a plastic trailer tail on the hook, can be deadly when lilted across the bottom like a jig-and-pig. At Wilson Lake, smallmouth will take silver slab spoons intended for white bass and nightcrawlers meant for walleye.

Wilson is the state's deepest, clearest and rockiest lake. It also holds the most smallmouth. Schools of the bronze bass can sometimes be located off rocky points that reach out toward the river channel, and around Rocktown Cove.

El Dorado supports a healthy population of smallmouth in its deeper waters off the dam face and off nearby rocky points. Milford Reservoir and the stilling basin below Webster Lake also hold smallmouth.

Chase and Clark State Fishing Lakes are rumored to hold smallmouth bass, but I don't know of anyone who has caught the species at either lake in recent years. Clark appears to have the depth, clarity and rocks that smallmouth prefer, but it may not be large enough to support many of the wide-ranging fish. Chase lies in the heart of spotted bass country, and I can't help but think the native species is better suited to its waters,

The Spring River system of extreme southeast Kansas may be the only waters that historically supported smallmouth bass before they were stocked elsewhere.

Because of the clean water they reside in, smallmouth taste better than largemouth, but they are also more vulnerable to being hurt by excess fishing pressure when not released.

A 15-inch length limit is more restrictive on smallmouth than on largemouth. Smallmouth don't grow as large and boast a stockier build, so they tend to be older and weigh more per inch. While the same length limit applies to all black bass on most lakes in the state, El Dorado features an 18-inch limit on largemouth and a 15-inch limit on smallmouth.

Besides a deeper, chunkier look, smallmouth feature vertical bars on their flanks, rather than the dark horizontal stripe of the largemouth. A line drawn straight up from its upper jaw would run through the pupil of its eye, while a line drawn from the upper jaw of a largemouth would run behind its eye.

Spring and fall are by far the best seasons for smallmouth fishing.

SPOTTED BASS
Still called "Kentucky" bass by many, the spotted was not recognized as a separate species until 1927, when it was thought to occur only in that state. Actually, its native range always included streams in the Flint Hills and southeast Kansas.

Looking something like a cross between a smallmouth and largemouth, the spotted bass is the smallest of Kansas' black bass species, in part because it lives in the harshest environment. Built lean and mean from contending with the constant current of streams, spotted bass fight especially hard — a 2½ pound spotted could pass for a 4-pound largemouth.

In the past 20 years, however, stream fishermen in eastern Kansas have been catching more and more largemouth and fewer and fewer spotted bass. Wildlife and Parks biologist Rick Tush believes human tinkering with stream systems is reducing the habitat for all fish while giving largemouth a competitive advantage over spotted bass.

An avid fishermen of streams near his home in Eureka, Tush explained that reservoirs and watershed dams have dramatically reduced the streams' seasonal ebbs and flows. Periodic floodwaters gouge holes in the riverbeds and undercut the banks, creating deep pools and hiding places for bass and other fish. Dams short-stop the floodwaters and stifle the streams. Silt that would've been flushed downstream in springtime floods, settles to the bottom instead, further filling in the deep spots.

Not only have the ponds, lakes and reservoirs reduced fish habitat in streams,

they have also been stocked with largemouth bass. When largemouth are stocked behind a dam in a river, they are, in effect, added to the stream system. Spotted bass are declining, in part, because the largemouth now greatly outnumber them in some waters.

Spotted bass continue to thrive in stream systems flowing through rocky grassland hills that have been altered little since the arrival of white settlers. Any submerged log, brushpile, bank undercut or shaded pool is likely to hold one and possibly several of the fish.

Lures that are especially effective on spotted bass include: small spinnerbaits, Beetlespins, plastic worms, hollow-bodied tube jigs and jigs with rubber tails and bodies that stretch over the head, such as Cabela's "Skinheads." Colors that seem to produce the most consistent action are: blue-and-chartreuse spinnerbaits, green-and-orange Beetlespins and sparkling blue worms and jigs. Jig-and-pigs can be excellent around brushpiles and undercuts in springtime.

Spotted bass have a blotchy lengthwise stripe that looks like a dark row of diamonds in some fish but is hard to see at all in others. Under this lateral line are rows of small, dark, closely spaced spots. Larger, light spots are sometimes visible along the back of stressed fish.

The end of a spotted bass' mouth extends to near the back of the eye, but not beyond it, leaving it between the largemouth and smallmouth, but leaning toward the latter.

Its behavior also tends to more closely resemble the smallmouth, as it prefers current to slow water, cool temperatures over warm, deep holes over shallow oxbows, and rocky structure over weedbeds. On the other hand, spotted and largemouth bass can be caught at opposite ends of the same log when they occur together in a stream.

SHORTLY AFTER DAWN on a morning in the middle of May, we anchored near Pelican Point on Wilson Lake. Hooking nightcrawlers through the nose, we lowered quarter-ounce jigs of flourescent orange. They sunk 37 feet, then hit bottom, the lines going slack. We pulled them up an inch – just enough to keep the line straight.

As usual, the walleye were nibbling cautiously. Bruce Coate felt two subtle licks against his line. He waited, concentrating intently.

The rod tip bent down slightly; the line moved. Coate set the hook, his light-action rod doubled over, and he reeled up a 3-pound walleye.

"It's unbelievable how many walleye are in this lake," Coate said. "I've seen nearly 700 caught out of this boat in the last 30 days."

Wilson is just one of many superb walleye lakes in Kansas. Lovewell, Kanopolis, Milford, Kirwin and Melvern Reservoirs consistently boast abundant walleye populations. Cheney, Marion and El Dorado Reservoirs offer excellent walleye fishing from time to time. State and community lakes periodically produce surprising numbers of the cloudy-eyed perch, though a heavy spring flood or a crush of spawning-season fishing pressure can quickly clean out a small body of water.

No reservoir in Kansas, and few on the Great Plains, offers better walleye habitat than Glen Elder, with its miles and miles of winding river channel. The lake attracted national attention in 1988 when

144 anglers caught 1,000 walleye — nearly a ton of fish — during a two-day tournament.

That tournament frightened many anglers and fisheries biologists into reexamining the state's generous walleye creel limit. Within a year, the daily limit was cut from 8 to 5. The new limit matched those of neighboring states and was strongly supported by the Kansas Walleye Association, which sponsors tournaments at state reservoirs throughout the spring and summer.

Tournament walleye fishing began a rapid surge in popularity in the late 1980s — due largely to heavy promotion by the *In-Fisherman* media network of Brainerd, Minnesota; the Mercury/Mariner corporation of Fond du Lac, Wisconsin; and other equipment manufacturers.

Elden Bailey has learned to disregard much of the walleye fishing information that has come to Kansas from up North, where the tasty fish swim in their native streams and glacial lakes. Bailey has been fishing Kansas reservoirs for walleye since the mid-1960s, when "people would laugh at you if you talked about it."

He won the first fishing tournament he entered, in 1968. He waited until 1981 to

enter his second tournament, but won that too. In '86 and '87, he teamed up with friend Gary Miller to take the first two state walleye tournament circuit titles.

"For years, all you heard was walleye won't go shallow, that sun hurt their eyes," Bailey said. "They tell you to fish rocks at night. Baloney. I'll tell you to fish mud in daytime."

Walleye roam in loose schools. Like most fish, they relate strongly to structure — dropoffs at points; river channels; gravel roads and railroad beds; humps and submerged islands; brushpiles in deep water and brushpiles at dropoffs.

"The only gadget on the market that'll help a walleye fisherman is a depth finder," Bailey said.

Peak walleye fishing season generally runs from early May through mid-June in Kansas, varying a week or two from year

Nightfish for walleye only during spring spawn. Otherwise, walleye feed from time to time throughout the day, rain or shine.

to year. This is when the fish hit lake mudflats to rut up the larvae of Mayflies and other insects and "anyone can catch walleye and every method you know will work," Bailey said.

A popular and effective way to locate walleye in Kansas is to drift with the wind across a stretch of flats that is fringed by points and broken up by channel switch-backs, humps, old road intersections and other holding structures.

Find out what depth the fish have been feeding in from bait shop operators, sporting goods dealers or other fisher-men. Ask what color has been attracting the most strikes: pink, red, blaze orange, yellow, chartreuse, green?

A colored jig head with a bare hook tipped with nightcrawler or leech works well drifted across the bottom. Some experts prefer maribou jigs. The wet feathering lays down neatly against a worm, they say, adding attractive color without distracting the fish from what's important. Others like jigs with rubber twister tails or complete rubber dressings to add color, flash and a soft touch that may convince a nibbling walleye to chomp down. Still others take a middle road, choosing maribou jigs with a bit of plastic on the hook shank.

"Floating" jig heads also work well with leeches and crawlers. So do worm harnesses and the various combinations of swivels, dipsy sinkers, leaders and hooks — known as Lindy Rigs, Wolf River Rigs and so on.

Keep the bait just above bottom, so that it bumps from time to time but rarely snags. Use light line — 4 to 8 pound test. The clearer the water, the clearer the line should be.

When you get a hit, mark the spot with a colorful weighted float. If you have a depthfinder, return to the area and search for a good walleye focus point, such as brush at a roadway intersection or a hump with steep slopes. Anchor and fish straight down, fluttering a baited jig or a slab spoon off the bottom. Or cast out

and reel slowly back, bouncing the lure up the dropoff, around the hump or in and out of the brushpile.

If there is too little or too much wind for drifting — 15 miles per hour is ideal — then you can troll against the wind or simply find likely structure and set anchor.

Small walleye of 2 pounds and under typically hit the mudflats earliest. Too young to participate fully in the energy-sapping spawn of March and early April, they don't suffer the post-breeding let down that seems to lock the jaws of large walleye for two weeks or more.

While young walleye sometimes hit baits with abandon, big fish tend to feed cautiously. When Bailey detects a light nibble, he slowly tilts his rod toward the fish, lending line without giving slack. He feels the pecking sensation of a walleye rolling the worm in its mouth, bouncing it against its teeth. At the instant he feels dead weight at the end of the line, he sets the hook.

Around the middle of June, sometimes a little earlier, young shad of the year have grown large enough to catch the walleyes' fancy, and they begin to turn their attention upward. Glen Elder fisheries biologist Ken McCloskey likes to demonstrate how a walleye watches overhead by pressing the head of a fish against his hand, as if it were rooting for insects in his palm. Its gill covers pop out and its eyes fold inward so that both are looking almost straight up.

When the fish start chasing shad, it's often easiest to locate them by trolling slender minnow lures, such as Shadlings and Rapalas.

"It happens when the white bass start really hitting the surface," McCloskey said.

In fact, you can often find walleye in June and July the same way you would find white bass and stripers — rising from dropoffs and river channels to gorge on small gizzard shad.

Nobody likes to tell fishing stories better than Bob Roberts, an avid angler from Salina — except when he is searching for shad schools at Kanopolis Reservoir. Then Roberts becomes a silent study in concentration as he circles his boat and stares at his depthfinder.

Once Roberts locates a mountain of shad, he tosses out a buoy marker and slowly trolls over the school. One morning, late in July, we were jigging chartreuse slab spoons with tiny spinner blades in 13 feet of water when Roberts called for the net. A healthy four-pound walleye came into the boat, followed quickly by another

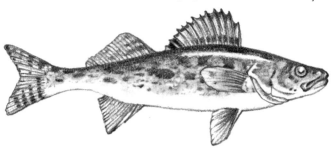

Walleye

of equal size. We had intended to catch white bass, thinking it too hot for decent mid-day walleye fishing.

That's a trademark of fishing shad schools in Kansas reservoirs, where many species prey upon young shad. You can catch walleye, white bass, stripers, drum and smallmouth in the same place at the same time.

Even in August, when walleye grow too lazy to chase trolled lures, "it's sure not impossible to catch a few nice fish," said Bailey.

Once again, slow drifting is a good way to locate fish, which will cluster in brush beside a channel, a road, a weedbed or other "edge."

"I like brush so thick that you have to use a ⅟₁₆-ounce or ⅛-ounce weedless jig," Bailey said. "You have to drop the jig right into the brush. I've caught limits out of places no bigger than a table top."

Walleye of four pounds and more feed much like large catfish in the heat of summer. In fact, Bailey once caught a 22½ pound channel cat while walleye fishing on a warm summer day. As usual, he was using 4-pound test.

It turned out to be a world line-test record.

Summer walleye generally bite best between 10 a.m. and 2 p.m., when wind and waves are stirring up bait while reducing visibility. This makes it easier to anchor directly over feeding fish without spooking them.

Walleye, especially big walleye, also bite well in the middle of the night. Shy, nighttime feeders are larger because they survive longer than fish that aggressively chase down food — and fishing lures — in daylight, McCloskey said..

"Big, big walleye are usually nighttime feeders and it takes a lot of hard work to catch them," said Coate. "I don't think people — including myself — are doing what it takes. Most of the biggest walleye probably die of old age."

Coate believes Wilson Lake's walleye habitat is too good not to harbor old fish in the 15-pound range, though the state record stands at 13.06.

The one time of year when anglers have no choice but to wait until dark to catch walleye is the spawning season, which begins in March and sometimes runs into early April. That's when the fish move into rocky, windswept shallows to spawn. One of the first gamefish species to stir each spring, walleye head for their breeding grounds when the surface temperature reaches 45 degrees.

In their native northern habitat, the fish swim upstream to spawn in shallow spots where a current flows over clear bottoms of gravel, stone and sand. In Kansas reservoirs, they congregate in spots where

When walleye are in a nibbling mood, they can steal dozens of nightcrawlers from a fishermen before he has a chance to set the hook. This is especially true in Kansas, where strong winds frequently bob rods and wiggle lines, making it difficult to detect light nibbles.

A guide I know adds a second hook to his jig-and-crawler to nab worm thieves — and his sting operation works very well.

First, tie on a jig. Next, take a snelled hook with three-inch leader and attach the leader to the eye of the jig. (Leader length can vary with the size of your bait.)

Put the jig hook through the nose of the nightcrawler, then straighten the worm out. Embed the second hook into the body of the nightcrawler so that it hangs almost straight down.

Walleye who have been adept at avoiding the first hook often get caught by the second.

waves roll over rocks, gravel and hard-packed clay (never mud). Rocky points and banks can be just as productive as dam rip-rap areas that receive heavy fishing pressure.

Anglers fishing the spawn should anchor within casting distance of the bank or wade into the water. Cast shallow-running lures on a line parallel with the rocks. Let crankbaits and spinners (any minnow imitation will do) bump bottom in 18 inches of water. Glen Elder anglers like to "foot troll" across the dam. They simply cast out a floating Rapala, hold the rod out over the water and walk down the dam face.

The April post-spawn period is the toughest time of year to catch sizeable fish. In years of high spring rains, heavy water releases by reservoirs flush many

spawning walleye into the spillways below the dams. Using a jig tipped with a minnow or nightcrawler, you can sometimes luck into good April fishing by casting upstream in the spillway, then letting the bait bounce naturally down with the current.

Because release rates at Kansas reservoirs are frequently high, state fisheries managers believed for many years that the species would not benefit from strict creel or length limits. If spawning fish were likely to be flushed out of the reservoir every few years, then anglers might as well be allowed to take advantage of good walleye populations when they existed, they reasoned.

Some walleye fishing experts and lake biologists never bought this theory, however. They argued that many large walleye spawned on rocky points far from dam outlets, where they were not in danger of being washed downstream.

In addition, they said, walleye are particularly vulnerable to excess fishing pressure because:

☞ They concentrate heavily in shallow, accessible waters during spawning season. They aggressively attack baits and lures when young.

☞ They have become the target species for a large and rapidly increasing number of competitive tournament fishermen.

☞ They are considered by many — perhaps most — freshwater anglers to be the finest tasting of fish. As a result, few walleye are released.

Indeed, limits of tiny, year-old walleye were commonly taken home by Lovewell Reservoir fishermen when those were the only fish remaining in the lake.

An experimental 18-inch length limit on walleye was imposed at Lovewell in 1988. Walleye size and numbers improved dramatically in the lake within three years. A 15-inch limit was applied at Glen Elder in 1990, while 18-inch limits were added at: Big Hill, Cedar Bluff, Cheney, El Dorado, Elk City, Hillsdale, La Cygne, Melvern and Pomona. Many Kansas Walleye Association members have strongly supported a statewide length limit of 18 inches.

As yet, there has been no research to show how well walleye survive being caught and released, according to McCloskey. Unlike largemouth bass — which anglers typically hook in the lip with artificial lures — walleye are caught mostly on live bait, which they sometimes swallow.

It's also unknown how many non-tournament anglers would accept catch-and-release walleye fishing.

For one thing, walleye range farther than largemouth bass or stream trout — the fish most likely to be caught and released at present. Toss a walleye back today and you won't catch it behind the same log or rock tomorrow — in fact, odds are you will never see the same fish again.

On top of that, a reservoir's walleye population will rise and fall naturally with spring water levels, albeit not as dramatically as state officials once maintained.

Most importantly, the walleye makes for spectacular table fare — tastier than trout and far, far more edible than largemouth bass.

My own guess is that catch-and-release fishing will continue to spread among expert walleye fishermen and those working to become experts. The majority of anglers, on the other hand, will prove most willing to release small "cigar" fish but will continue to keep any walleye of two pounds or more, no matter how much the tournament fishermen lobby and cajole.

SAUGER/SAUGEYE

Though rare in Kansas today, the walleye's next of kin could become common if experimental stockings at Melvern and Council Grove reservoirs prove successful.

Prized as both a sport and food fish,

sauger look much like walleye, but sport dark, saddlelike blotches on the back and sides, plus rows of small dark spots on the dorsal fin.

They tend to grow smaller than walleye — sauger seldom reach 4 pounds and the world record weighed 8 pounds, 12 ounces. The world-record walleye weighed 25 pounds.

Sauger do grow and mature rapidly, however, reaching a length of 13 inches by age two (as compared to 18 inches by age four).

Once native to the Marais des Cygnes River system in eastern Kansas, sauger disappeared after the impoundment of Lake of the Ozarks in Missouri.

About one million sauger fry were stocked in Melvern Reservoir, at the head of the Marais des Cygnes, in 1988. Long a producer of big walleye, Melvern's population had suffered in recent years due to turbid water and heavy springtime dam releases, said Gene Ploskey, Wildlife and Parks research fisheries biologist.

Because sauger tolerate muddy, turbid water better than walleye, state fisheries experts thought the species might prove better suited to Melvern.

In addition, thousands of saugeye fingerlings have been stocked in Council Grove, a shallow reservoir with heavy release rates that also has seen a drop in walleye numbers in recent years. Saugeye, of course, are the hybrid offspring of walleye and sauger.

If either sauger or saugeye do well, they may be stocked in other reservoirs, state lakes and community lakes where walleye survival has been hampered by muddy water or by heavy flushing during March and April, when many walleye congregate around dam riprap to spawn .

Creel, length and possession limits for sauger and saugeye are the same as those for walleye.

ALTHOUGH YOU can't get much farther from the sea than Kansas, the state's waters harbor three members of the sea bass family. A freshwater natural, the white bass is smallest of the three and the only native Kansan. A saltwater native, the huge striper arrived in the 1960s. And hopes remain high that the

wiper, a hybrid offspring of the two, may yet turn out to be the most popular sea bass of all among Kansas anglers.

STRIPERS

If they hadn't built Santee-Cooper Dam in South Carolina back in 1941, there wouldn't be striped bass in Kansas today. When the dam gates first closed, stripers that had migrated upriver to spawn were blocked from returning to the Atlantic Ocean. Instead of dying, they flourished in Lakes Marion and Moultrie, the two huge impoundments formed by Santee-Cooper.

Stocked in impoundments from state to state, stripers have become the glory fish of reservoirs throughout the southern half of the nation. In a few places, such as Lake Texoma in southern Oklahoma, they manage to reproduce naturally.

Stripers cannot sustain their own populations in Kansas, however, and must be restocked from year to year in Cheney, Glen Elder and Wilson lakes.

For many years, stripers thrived in all three impoundments, feeding on ample supplies of gizzard shad and growing to 20, 30 and 40 pounds. In recent summers, Cheney's big stripers have died off as

siltation has decreased the reservoir's depth and structure, leading to higher turbidity and summer water temperatures.

Striper numbers have remained healthy in Glen Elder, but they don't tend to reach great size, as the lake is fairly shallow and heavily fished.

As a result, Wilson may be the only place in Kansas to catch huge striped bass for years to come. It has produced the last two state records — a 42 pounder in 1986 and a 43.5 pounder in 1988. And when the latest record was caught, at least one bigger fish still lurked in the lake depths, according to Bruce Zamrzla, Wilson Lake fisheries biologist.

Zamrzla knew because he had caught the larger fish in his own test nests just one week before he helped Chet Nily weigh in the new record. Fearful of killing the monster striper if he handled it too much, Zamrzla freed it from the test net without weighing it. He did weigh a 32-pounder from the same net, however.

And it appeared to Zamrzla that the smaller fish could have slipped right down the giant's mouth.

Zamrzla's test catch only adds to the growing mystique about Kansas' deepest lake and its stripers. Stop by Bud George's bait shop, which overlooks the northeast corner of the lake, and you can gaze upon his 42-pound striper, which takes up a goodly portion of one wall. A state record in its time, it is the kind of fish a man chases for years before he finally pulls it from the water (if he ever pulls it from the water).

George couldn't get to sleep one night in June, 1986. They say up Wilson way that the fish was calling out to him, issuing its challenge. He got out of bed at 2:30 in the morning, took his boat onto the dark lake waters and set out his lures.

Their battle didn't end until the sun came up.

"This lake has always been underrated for its fishing," said fulltime Wilson guide Bruce Coate. "Big fish are a different animal to catch than small fish."

Anglers in Coate's boat alone catch between 1,000 and 1,400 stripers per year.

When hunting for stripers, Coate plies Wilson's waters with outriggers as well as downriggers, much like a Great Lakes charter captain trolling after salmon and trout.

As the names suggest, an outrigger carries lures out 50, even 75 feet to the side of the boat, while a downrigger carries lures to the depths.

A downrigger weight, attached by cable to a stern-mounted winch, is connected to the fishing line by a rubber band or by a light clamp (available through catalog fishing outfitters). When the weight is cranked down, it takes the lure with it — as deep as 70 feet in a lake such as Wilson. After lowering the weight and lure to the desired depth, you reel in all slack and continue reeling until you've put a deep bend in the rod.

When a fish bites, it breaks the band or

pulls the line free of the clothespin clamp. Once the fishing line is released of the heavy downrigger weight, the rod pops up, automatically setting the hook and signalling the fisherman of a bite.

An outrigger sled also runs on its own cable and is attached the same way to a fishing line. As the sled is cranked out, its keel pulls the lure away from the boat. The lure runs at the same depth as it would if simply cast behind the boat and trolled.

"This has been used very, very little in the middle United States," Coate said. "Outriggers are good on clear-water days,

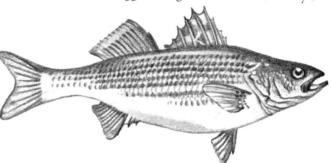

Striped Bass

especially in springtime, when the fish are very spooky. It keeps lures away from the boat, which scares them."

Outriggers can be especially effective on a shallow lake like Cheney, where stripers are easily frightened by boat motors overhead.

When fish are attacking aggressively, lures can be attached close to downrigger weights, trailing only six or eight feet behind. A hungry striper rising to inspect a weight will be more likely to see and attack a lure that's close by.

Conversely, when fish are sluggish or skittish, it's best to trail lures 30 to 40 feet behind the weights. If the water is clear, Coate sometimes moves the lures far as 100 feet back, to reduce chances of spooking fish with the weight or the boat.

Big stripers bite best from early May to mid-June and from mid-October to late

November, when the water temperature falls below 65 degrees.

In May, stripers roam 30 to 50 feet down all day long, then suddenly rise in the evening to hammer surfacing schools of shad. Shallow-running lures, pulled by downriggers, will often pick off fish as they rise from dropoffs.

By late June, stripers are cruising around the deep half of a reservoir, spending most of their time in cooler depths. The big fish tend to hang around river channels and humps in their travels, favoring spots where they can rise quickly into shallow water to ambush prey. Top spots for action include humps with steep dropoffs, points approaching stream channels and old roadbeds that stripers can follow from a channel to a bank.

In fall, stripers return to springtime patterns until the lake is uniformly cool.

"When the water's the same temperature from top to bottom, stripers could be anywhere, just like white bass," Coate said.

In fact, ice fishermen often catch stripers along with white bass while jigging spoons, Kastmasters and other lures resembling falling or fluttering shad.

Coate uses only clear fishing line on wary stripers; Wilson boasts unusually high visibility for a Kansas lake. He trolls long minnow lures, such as Storm "Big Macs" and Rebels. He also uses homemade jigs of 1½ ounces with long fliptails. He trolls at about four knots in the summer months, two knots in the spring and fall.

When fishing between 18 and 25 feet, he likes the colors black and silver. Between 30 and 40 feet, he prefers white and blue with pink trailers. Under low-light conditions, he switches to black.

Coate fished in national striper tournaments for 10 years, nearly always placing in the top 10, before starting his Wilson guiding service in the mid-1980s. He always tries to fish above stripers, never below.

"They're constructed to look up," he says. "One time in Tennessee, I saw a striper on my graph rise from 60 feet deep to take a lure at 22 feet. But they're never going to dive down after one."

On lazy days, he uses ingenious tricks to lure stripers to strike.

When his sonar shows fish suspended along the side of a channel, for example, Coate will sometimes drop a "school of shad" on top of them. He ties a three-way swivel to each of four lines. To one eye of each swivel, he ties an 18-inch leader holding a 1½-ounce jig with tail. To the other eye, he ties a 4-foot leader holding a ¾-ounce jig with tail.

The light jig rides above and behind the heavy one, like two shad swimming through the water. With all four downriggers holding tandem jigs at the same depth, Coate trolls across the channel holding spot, then shifts into neutral.

As the boat stops moving forward, the eight "shad" flutter downward into the channel toward the waiting wolves.

"Sometimes the stripers just can't resist a falling bait," Coate says. "It'll get you fish when nothing else will."

Every August, for two weeks or so, striped bass rise briefly at dawn on Glen Elder Reservoir to slash into surfacing schools of shad. Tossing buzz baits and other surface lures into the feeding frenzy, you're likely to lose more fish than you catch. Use a stiff bass rod with heavy test line. Check your drag before casting. And don't fall out of the boat!

Although stripers spend most of their time in deep water, they can be reached from shore. Nily caught his state record from a point on Wilson Lake, using a white bass for bait. Stripers will typically rise from the depths of a channel to the shallows off a point to feed at night.

Add shorefishing tackle and a touch of imagination and Cheney Lake begins to look and act like an inlet of the sea. Just ask old salt Andy McMinn, a retired sailor and co-founder of the Southern

Kansas Striper Association in Wichita.

McMinn and other Cheney shore fishermen wade out into waist-deep water, rear back their 15-foot surf rods and cast out rigs featuring three-ounce to eight-ounce sinkers and two hooks baited with cut shad. They slowly reel out line while walking back to shore, then set the high poles in holders anchored in the sand.

McMinn owns an 18-foot boat complete with downriggers, flashers and a paper sonar recorder. But he doesn't use it much.

"When you're out in a boat, you don't see as much — at least I don't see as much," he said. "You're always working and fooling with gadgets; you don't see the owls, the waterfowl, the sunsets. Last Tuesday I was out here and didn't catch a thing. But I heard two hoot owls — one would hoot and then the other hooted back. Then a turkey started gobbling in between them. And I started watching the mud hens — I had no idea how comical they can be. When I'm done, I just pack up the rods and the lawnchair and go home. I just think it's a lot more interesting this way."

The striper is an Atlantic relative of the freshwater white. Wipers are their hybrid offspring.

McMinn says he catches more stripers from shore than he does in his boat. He also catches white bass, walleye and channel cats with his long, light-action rods.

In addition to sending cut baits all the way out to the river channels underlying Cheney Reservoir, the thin-tipped surf rods add lively movement to cut baits and help entice stripers to strike, McMinn says.

He keeps a log that helps him figure out which point to cast from, depending on the season, the temperature, the wind and other factors. A couple of randomly chosen excerpts reveal some of the finer points about Cheney shore fishing:
☞ Oct. 26, Sunday, 6:30-8:30 a.m. Heimermann Point. Misty, windy, 10-20 NNE, 44-50 degrees, 9-pound striper and 1 white bass. Water getting colder. Few ducks moving about lake, 1 large crane in shallows along shoreline. Lots of rabbits out. Beautiful morning and hot coffee was a treat.

☞ Nov. 10, Monday, Cheney Refuge Island and north side of Wichita Point. Cloudy, misty, 28 degrees, wind 35 gusting to 45. Reels freezing, 7 whites, 1 walleye, channel. Kept 1 stripers about 6 pounds to eat and released three more. Fishing red-hot, weather ice-cold. Made coffee — drank entire 14-cup pot. Waders leaking again.

Chest waders — preferably a pair that don't leak — are a requirement for bank fishing during cool-water months. Though some dropoffs can be reached by casting from the bank without walking in the water, an angler battling a hooked striper often must wade out a few yards to steer fish away from shoreline trees and scrub.

An effective bait rig for catching stripers from shore includes a heavy weight at the end of the line (the lighter the rod action, the lighter the sinker). About six inches up from the sinker, attach a three-inch leader with a large hook. Another 2½ feet up the line, attach a second leader and hook. Channel catfish often take the lower bait.

When a striper hits, the rod tip bounces with abandon. Even a little six-pounder provides great sport, in part because you have so much line out.

McMinn had high hopes of catching a state-record striper from the banks of Cheney until September, 1989, when stripers ranging from 15 to more than 30 pounds started washing up on the lake's shores.

Nearly all of Cheney's big stripers died from temperature stress after a summer that stayed too hot for too long, according to lake biologist Gordon Schneider.

"Large stripers over 11 or 12 pounds can't tolerate water temperatures above 75 degrees for extended periods," Schneider says. "They don't eat, they lose weight, until they finally starve to death."

As Cheney Reservoir continues to grow more shallow and muddy with age, its average water temperature rises, making it less suitable for trophy stripers.

"The lake has less volume of storage, so it tends to warm up faster," Schneider said. "The lake is also more turbid than it was, and a colored lake warms up faster than a clear lake."

Heat stress in aging freshwater impoundments, plus pollution in the Chesapeake Bay and other East Coast striper breeding areas, have led to reductions in striper stocking in recent years. Many experts hope that hybrid wipers will be able to pick up the slack.

"Wipers are the hot fish across the country," said Tommie Crawford, manager of the Milford State Fish Hatchery. "They've got good size — not quite as big as stripers — and they're more adaptable to our climate."

WIPERS

Like mules, wipers are hybrid beasts which combine admirable traits of the big striper (horse) and the little white bass (donkey). To compare sizes, the state record striper weighed 43½ pounds, the state record white weighed 5¼ pounds, while the state record wiper weighed in at nearly 19 pounds. Wipers should be able to grow to a maximum size of about 20 pounds in Kansas, according to biologists.

The original recipe for making wipers called for crossing a female striper with a male white bass. Striped bass and white bass are distant relatives, with stripers evolving along sea coasts while whites took to freshwater streams. Under natural conditions, stripers leave saltwater to reproduce, making spring spawning runs up rivers flowing into the ocean.

Striped bass produce larger eggs than white bass, and larger eggs are easier for biologists to handle in the artificial spawning grounds of a fish hatchery.

"The original hybrid is ideal to work with, but across the country, there's been a lot of trouble coming up with striped bass

Wipers have stripes too and can be hard to tell apart from whites until they grow large.

females," Crawford says. "So we've been turning to reciprocal hybrids, where you switch the parents around."

Using white bass females poses unique problems, however, for their small eggs clump together like tapioca pudding. "This increases the risk for fungus and you lose a lot of eggs and fry," Crawford says.

While some states have experimented with tannic acid to separate white bass eggs, with mixed results, Crawford came up with a new idea in 1988. Since white bass reproduce successfully in muddy Kansas lakes, he thought, perhaps a solution of clay and water would keep the eggs from clumping. His first test hatch produced 2.5 million wiper fry for stocking in Pomona, Milford, Kirwin, Sebelius and Webster reservoirs.

Wiper fry produced from white bass eggs also are smaller than fry produced from striper eggs and have less chance for survival. Crawford hopes eventually to re-

White Bass

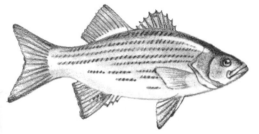

lease some fry into state rearing ponds in an effort to raise intermediate-sized wipers that can be stocked after reaching several inches in length. Wildlife and Parks enjoyed an excellent wiper production year in 1990, and the number of lakes receiving the fish jumped dramatically.

Hybrids produced from female white bass eventually turn out to be identical to wipers produced from female stripers.

"They start out smaller, but their long-term growth is the same," Crawford says. "Basically, you can't tell them apart."

Like stripers, wipers can't reproduce naturally and must be stocked from year to year. They have done very well in older Kansas reservoirs, such as Kanopolis, and may prove ideally adapted for shallow lakes with thriving gizzard shad populations, including Cheney, El Dorado and many state fishing lakes.

Wipers behave much like white bass. They are caught using the same methods, and are hard to distinguish from whites until they surpass them in size. Wipers have stripes along the sides, like striped bass, but the lines are usually broken. Wipers have a larger head and more elongated shape than the hump-backed whites.

Until 1989, there was no limit on wipers because of the difficulty in telling them apart from white bass. This discouraged some biologists from stocking the hybrids, for fear they could be quickly fished out, unlike whites, which can reproduce prolifically to fill the carrying capacity of a lake. A daily limit of two wipers now applies statewide, making it important for anglers to know the difference.

WHITES

Scrappy white bass provide some of Kansas' most furious fishing. Schooling whites can be found year round, but the best fishing often arrives early in the year. In April, when the water temperature

Fast and furious white bass fishing arrives in April, when the fish head upstream of many reservoirs to spawn.

for commotion caused by white bass surfacing after shad — gulls and terns often give the whites away. Toss a silver spinner or a crankbait that imitates shad into the feeding school. If the whites have disappeared before you arrive, jig slab spoons just off the bottom in the same spot.

Use the same methods after locating a school of shad with a depth finder, snapping jigs, slabs or spoons such as Little Cleos and Kastmasters off the bottom. Chartreuse, silver and white are good colors. Some days it helps to add a strip of blue or orange tape to a silver spoon. On other days, a tiny propeller blade on the end of a slab seems to draw attention.

White bass often hang in schools at the end of points, in 10 to 20 feet of water, though they will follow shad anywhere and everywhere.

Ice fishing in Kansas generally means white bass fishing, though stripers, wipers, crappie, walleye and channel catfish also remain active year-round. Whites sometimes hammer a spoon jigged through the ice, but also often feed very cautiously when the water is cold: a tiny vibration, or slowly drifting line could signal a bite.

A community of ice fishermen commonly forms wherever the whites are biting. You also would do well to check out the points, dropoffs and humps that produce whites consistently in summertime.

reaches into the 50s, whites head upstream of many impoundments to spawn. Jigs cast across the stream and bounced back across the bottom — including jigs with spinners (e.g. Road Runners) — work especially well on spawning whites.

Slab spoons, spinners and anything else resembling small shad work well throughout the year. Watch lake surfaces

A FAIR SHARE of today's fishermen got hooked on the sport as youngsters reeling in bluegill, sunfish and crappie — including Bill Harmon of Durham. ❧ Fact is, Bill never has stopped fishing for the tasty little scrappers, except maybe when the stripers, largemouth or white bass happen to be biting better.

You can see Harmon's strong sense of priorities in the sign on his refrigerator: "Fishing is not just a matter of life or death, it's much more important than that."

A retired chief master sergeant, Harmon remains more active than a typical teenager by painting houses, writing outdoor stories, attending night school and fishing, fishing, fishing, fishing. Oh, and he hunts a little, too.

Thanks to the Air Force, Harmon fished around much of the world before returning to Kansas and settling in his wife's hometown, at the upper end of Marion lake. Along the way, he taught his favorite sport to countless pupils and picked up more than his share of stories.

He claims that days spent fishing will relieve headaches, soften heartaches, mend broken bones and cure baldness. He takes great pains to keep himself healthy, happy and hairy.

During one recent winter, from November to February, Harmon and friends caught more than 2,000 crappie at Council Grove Reservoir. Many of the fish weighed more than two pounds.

"I'd tell the guys, 'OK, get ready, they're 10 feet off the bottom,' and they lifted up their jigs and began catching them like crazy," he recalled. "Sometimes, they'd be schooled up off the front and back of the boat and not in the middle. Sometimes they'd be just off the front or just off the back."

"Yeah," added Irvin Christiansen, a frequent fishing partner of Harmon. "I'd be catching fish off my end and he wouldn't be catching any. Then, all of a sudden, he'd start catching 'em and I wouldn't. I'd look around and say, "Hey, this isn't where I was.'"

"And I'd tell him, 'That's right. When you've got a $14,000 boat, you put it wherever you want to,'" Harmon said with a boyish grin.

In early spring, when crappie spawn in shallow water, Harmon follows the banks closely, watching his depthfinder for brushpiles, sudden dropoffs, or an irregular bottom.

He starts in very shallow water with a bobber and jig. Harmon uses ultralight spinning gear and 6- to 8-pound test line. He prefers jigs of white, yellow and chartreuse, with a maribou tail.

"If big crappie are the rule, use large jigs, or match the available bait," he said. "Set the hook at the slightest twitch."

It's difficult to describe just how slight a twitch Harmon is referring to. It's a twitch that inexperienced fishermen can rarely detect. Skilled crappie fishermen often pull in four or five fish for every one caught by a less-seasoned angler.

Keep a finger on the line and watch it closely. Most strikes occur while the jig is still or on the fall. Miss it and you rarely get a second chance.

"If the line becomes slack, set the hook," he said. "If you just think something is there, set it."

Harmon also likes to wade into cattails after spring crappie. He uses a medium-light graphite pole, four feet of line and a rubber jig.

He eases into an area, drops the jig to the bottom, then raises it one inch. He jigs the pole and holds still. Standing in the same spot, he plunks the lure beside as many cattails as possible before moving.

"Don't spend more than five minutes in one area," he said. "If they're there, they'll bite."

Crappie spawning activity can suddenly cease. One day, you might be nailing them in six-inch shallows, the next day the crappie could be chasing shad through water 20 feet deep.

In a lake with high crappie numbers, such as Council Grove, Harmon looks for schools of shad after the spawn, locating them with a depth finder.

"Keep looking until you find fish before trying," he said. "In summer, work deeper dropoffs with brushpiles. Using your trolling motor, hold over the top of the piles and work the jig down inside the brush, keeping your finger on the line to get the feel of the brush. A heavier jig works better — a quarter-ounce — to drop the lure off of hangups."

Once Harmon finds a likely spot, he uses two jig sticks with different colored lures to tempt crappie into striking.

Easy-going Harmon is generous with both his fishing knowledge and his honey

holes. If he is catching buckets full of crappie and spots anglers who are striking out in a nearby boat, he often calls them over, ties their boat up to his and shares the fun.

"Man, that's all I'm out here for — to have a good time," he said.

FOR KIDS, FUN MEANS SIMPLE

You've got to be especially careful to keep that primary objective of having fun in focus at all times when starting kids fishing.

Keep everything as simple as you can. Head to areas where you expect the panfishing action to be hot and heavy. Cut your trip short if the fish stop biting or the child begins to lose interest.

Kids get hooked on pan fishing at an early age, so long as you keep things simple. Concentrate on having fun.

Some of us learned these common-sense lessons the hard way. I'll never forget one early spring trip to a lake west of Wichita with my oldest son, Nick, then just a two-year-old toddler.

As I unloaded the car trunk, Nick hopped up and down, taking swipes at anything that I carelessly dangled within range.

"Let me carry something!" he shouted. "Let me! Let me!"

Balancing the gear overhead, I smiled serenely and managed for upwards of 10 seconds to ignore his impassioned pleas. Then my new graphite rod began slipping from its perch between the cooler and the worm bucket.

Nick's eyes widened as the rod tip teetered closer to the ground. He pounced, grasping the tip tightly with both hands. Responding instinctively, I dropped everything to lunge for the falling rod handle and quickly found myself locked in battle with a 35-pound monster.

The rod doubled over as I hauled the lunker in. He fought ferociously, throwing in a number of acrobatic leaps while shouting: "No, no, it's mine! MIIINE!"

I finally worked him within reach, snatched him up by the collar, pried him from the pole and released him. Then I paused to catch my breath and loosen the kinks in my shoulders and forearms.

Once rested, I went to gather up the gear and lunch treats strewn across the ground. When I looked up a moment

Black Crappie

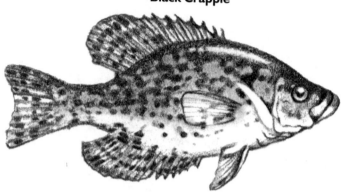

later, my firstborn was 30 yards away and running at full gallop, a large bag of Cheetos in his arms.

"Get back here!" I calmly suggested.

Nick glanced back, then tumbled on top of the cheese that went crunch, bursting the bag and scattering yellow curls like shrapnel. An alert flock of ducks waddled up from the lakeshore, quacking ecstatically as they engulfed the cheese puffs.

After retrieving my son from amid the ducks, I shut the car trunk and gathered up the fishing stuff. Half an hour had passed since we'd parked the car and we were finally off to the lake.

At a fishy looking spot along the bank, I shrugged off the gear, rigged and baited Nick's line and tossed it out. His bobber floated to rest about 10 yards from shore.

"I want to throw it! I want to throw it!" said the apple of my eye, reeling in frantically while I bent to pick up my rod.

"It's stuck! It's stuck!" he shouted as I threaded my line through the first eyelet on my rod.

Sure enough, his hook was deeply, al-

most permanently, embedded in a shoreline shrub. "Dad will have that fixed in no time," I said.

Twenty minutes later, his dad finally freed the hook. I found a new worm and cast back out. The bobber landed 20 yards away.

"Here's your pole, buddy," I said.

Nick didn't hear me. He was busy tossing a handful of loose bobbers into the lake. "I'm going to catch lots of fish," he explained.

I set down his rod and waded out after the bobbers. By the time I'd rounded all of them up, Nick was sitting beside the tackle box, carefully hooking together the last few links in a lengthy chain of plugs, spoons and spinners. "I make a big snake," he said, grinning.

I ran over, untangled the mess, led Nick back to his rod and put it in his hands. Then I picked up my own rod and threaded the line through the next eyelet. I was about to reach the third eyelet when he tugged at my pantleg, then pointed to a bush on the bank. His hook and bobber dangled in the branches.

With the sensitivity of a dentist yanking wisdom teeth, I extracted his hook, put on another worm, cast, then watched as the bobber sailed down about 40 yards from shore.

I stomped back over to my rod, only to find the line tangled in a crow's nest where I dropped it. Behind me, Nick was purposely reeling his hook in toward the shrub.

On the way home, Nick said, "Fishing's fun. But I don't catch any fish."

I beamed with pride. He was a chip off the old block.

Despite that poorly planned introduction, Nick quickly became a skillful and avid panfisherman. I learned to keep things down to the bare essentials, to guide him every step of the way, but also to let him actively participate in whatever ways he could. Nick learned to hook a nightcrawler, cast it out, watch the bobber and reel in fish, keeping his tip up and his line taut.

He even learned how to re-lease a fish unharmed to the wa-ter by holding the hook shank with a pliers and shaking it.

He learned a great deal in one evening about catching bluegills from shore, using techniques from the Old World, while fishing with 10-year-old Roy Keyes and his father, Mike, at Watson Lake Park in central Wichita.

Keyes was able to find fun and furious fishing in a wrung-out urban puddle after seeing how Europeans continue to enjoy tired streams and lakes that have been flailed at by fishermen for a thousand years.

He believes many American anglers

Yellow Perch

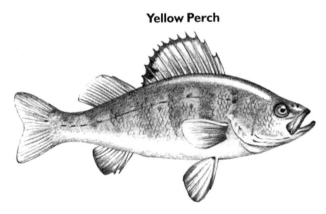

could enjoy better fishing by learning more about European ways. After all, he argues, America is becoming more like the Old World every year in terms of human popu-lation, fishing pressure and water quality.

"They haven't gotten into electronic fishing over there, they've just made bank

fishing very sophisticated," he says.

You aren't likely, for instance, to find red-and-white plastic balls bobbing on the

Bluegill

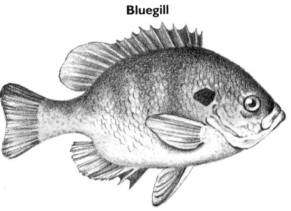

English streams once favored by Izaak Walton. Walton, who as a young man might have witnessed the debut perfor-mances of Shakespeare's plays, wrote the first English how-to guide to sportfishing from streams banks in the 1600s.

Europeans have been getting better at bank fishing ever since.

Their tools include very long, sensitive poles; lightweight lines; dainty hooks and various streamlined balsa floats — some for rough water, others for calm, some for casting, others for pitching, some to keep bait shal-low, others to hold it deep.

So light that they won't even slow down a bluegill, the floats behave less like typical American bobbers than like sensitive fly-line strike indicators.

The baits are worked much like flies as well. Keyes prefers maggots — live fly larvae — which are raised by the ton for English anglers, but seldom used here. Maggots come in five colors to help fishermen match insect hatches and adjust for sunlight and water clarity.

On an evening fishing trip, Roy Keyes demonstrated his bluegill catching ability by lightly pinching a maggot and hooking it through the lip. He swung out his 14-foot pole and settled the float over a sandy flat where the bluegill were congregating for their spring spawn.

The float twitched. Roy set the hook and swung in a fish. He released the fish easily, having earlier blunted the hook barbs with a pliers, then set out the float again. It dipped the instant it hit the water.

In three hours of after-school fishing, Roy caught 60 or so bluegill, an average spring evening.

A year earlier, Roy had caught a 14-pound carp on his light European gear at Lake Afton. His father had caught a 19-pounder on four-pound test line.

"Lake Afton is a carp fisherman's paradise," Roy said.

That's another thing, Keyes said: most American fishermen still look with disdain upon carp as unwanted foreigners that foul streams for "real" gamefish. It's more fun, he said, to accept the carp where their presence is irreversible, and to pursue them as sport fish with light gear.

Besides bluegill and carp, Keyes catches trout, crappie, catfish and even largemouth bass with his long poles and "microlight" tackle.

Keyes bought hundreds of dollars of shorefishing gear on a recent trip to Europe, where bank fishing can be an intensely competitive tournament sport, he said. Graphite poles run up to 45 feet long and can cost more than $2,000, he said.

On the other hand, you can probably still find a perfectly adequate 14-foot fiberglass crappie pole on sale at a local sport shop, and rig it with line, hook, float, BB weights and maggot, for less than $20.

Keyes buys most of his bait and equipment through Class Tackle, a Louisiana catalog outfitter boasting a complete line of European panfishing gear. Write for the Wazp Products catalog, P.O. Box 837, Minden, Louisiana 71055.

Crappies, bluegill and other sunfish can be caught year-round. The fastest action comes in springtime, when the fish move into very shallow water and aggressively defend their spawning areas.

Techniques for catching the fish are similar, although crappie like minnows better than the worms preferred by most other panfish.

Kansas enjoys both white and black crappie, with few differences between the two outside of their shade. Black crappie tend to be a tad larger than whites. Crappie swim in schools, often gathering around trees and other structure. When you catch one, stay in the same spot as others are near. Along with walleye, crappie are widely considered among the finest tasting freshwater fish.

Crappie rarely top three pounds, although the state record black weighed 4.63 pounds and the state's top white weighed 4.02. The world record black weighed six pounds, while the world record white weighed 5.19.

When crappie fishing is fast, small jigs or spinners are preferable to live bait simply because you can more quickly return an unbaited lure to the water. Anglers should make certain their jigs hang perpendicular to the line, like suspended minnows in the water; jigs should not dangle limply downward at the end of the line. Tie an improved clinch knot at the center of the jig eyelet and readjust as needed.

Bobbers with stop knots can be very helpful when fishing for any type of panfish. Tied with a separate, six-inch length of light monofilament line, the stop knot should be small enough to pass through the rod guides. Attach the knot where you want the bobber to stop. It should be tight enough to hold steady, but loose enough to slide to a new position if you wish to change depths.

After casting, the float will slip to the knot, suspending baits at the desired depth.

During springtime, you can often locate the spawning grounds of bluegill and redear sunfish by looking for plate-sized circles in the shallows. Male fish clear these nests, then wait for females to come in and spawn.

The fish aggressively defend their territories from their neighbors, flaring gill patches and constantly twitching and darting to meet intruders face to face. Flyfishing can be especially effective at this time, as the fish attack the trespassing insect.

Casting into a nesting area is better than trying to fish directly over one, where you risk spooking the bluegill away.

Worms are a favorite bluegill bait — bits of nightcrawler often work as well as whole worms. Any small, live bait found along the bank, including grasshoppers or crickets found under shoreline rocks, will catch sunfish.

Green sunfish grow fast in Kansas ponds and streams, where they can usually be found in shallow areas loaded with cover vegetation. Dangling a small spinner or rubber jig among the branches of a snag often yields numerous sunfish as well as an occasional bass.

Flyfishing with dry flies, poppers and nymphs also works well on green sunfish.

THERE ARE a thousand or more types of catfish roaming the world's waters. Two rank among the top gamefish species in Kansas: channel cats and flatheads. Both are smooth-skinned bottom dwellers with eight barbels, or whiskers, around the mouth. The whiskers actually are sophisticated smelling organs, as catfish track down much of their food by odor, unlike most gamefish, which respond primarily to sight and sound stimuli.

While it often pays to keep moving from point to point in a body of water until you find actively feeding fish, you should generally keep the bait in one place when after catfish and give the bloodhounds of the deep time to find you.

All catfish have sharp, stiff spikes at the lead edge of their back and side fins; they should be handled with care. Both flatheads and channel cats boast firm, mild meat, making them fine table fare.

That's where similarities end between the species, which are pursued, for the most part, by different groups of fishermen using distinctive methods and baits.

CHANNEL CATS

Some anglers focus on catfish, others groan whenever a catfish takes their bait. If ever the twain meet, it is over the channel cat.

Sleekest and most sporting of the continent's 35 species of catfish and bullhead, the channel cat also tends to frequent cleaner, swifter waters. They like deep holes, but also gentle currents, which explains why anglers have long associated them with stream channels.

Besides the worms, cut bait and stink baits used to catch any catfish, channel cats will strike dry flies and bass lures. They are becoming increasingly valuable as a commercially raised restaurant food fish.

Bluish gray, with a forked tail, white belly and black dots along the back and sides, channel cats average between two and five pounds, but the state record weighed 33¾ pounds and the world record weighed 58.

Most state reservoirs, fishing lakes and community lakes boast high channel catfish populations, which fishermen barely scratch, despite a generous creel limit of 10 daily.

America's most popular gamefish may be the largemouth bass, but it is by no means the favorite of every angler. Just ask Brent Hopkins, owner of Fish and Ski Marine in Wichita, who grew up fishing almost exclusively for largemouth with his father, Ron, a longtime state wildlife commissioner and tournament bass fisherman.

Brent prefers channel catfish over largemouth — or any other species Kansas has to offer.

"Bass fishing is competitive," he says. "You might catch two all day or you might catch 20. If you're not in the front of the boat, you don't catch as many. With channel catfish, you get a limit on all but the real bad days. They put up as hard a fight or harder. It's easier to catch more of them. It's something the family can enjoy — my 4-year-old can catch them.

Hopkins catches a limit nearly every trip out. Fishing up to four nights a week in summer and fall, he and his partners typically find themselves culling fish hours before they are through — returning smaller fish to the lake to make room for larger ones in the livewell.

"On an average night, two guys will bring home 20 catfish weighing three to four pounds apiece," he says.

That's another nice thing about channel cats — you can bring home supper without feeling guilty about not releasing the fish alive.

Wildlife and Parks fisheries biologists consider channel cats to be an "under-utilized resource" at many reservoirs, including Glen Elder and Hopkin's favorite — El Dorado — where 18-inch largemouth and walleye length limits have been imposed to protect declining populations.

At El Dorado, Hopkins starts drift-fishing the mud flats for channel cats as soon as the water warms up enough for him to catch shad in six-foot casting nets. In springtime, he locates shad schools with a depthfinder, then casts the weighted bait net over his shoulder. It drifts to the bottom, covering part of the school. As he pulls up the net, it closes, capturing the fish.

The large net enables him to catch shad in 15 feet of water early in the year. By mid-July, baitfish usually can be found in a couple feet of water, where a 3½ foot net works just as well.

After putting the shad on ice, Hopkins heads for a pair of pastures that were flooded over when El Dorado was formed. Although catfish can be caught anywhere on the reservoir, Hopkins prefers drifting over the pasture mudflats because they contain few snags.

"I don't like tying hooks at night," he says.

Fishing tends to be best between 7 p.m. and midnight, especially when the moon is dark. Catfish don't bite well under a full moon.

Unlike many catfishermen, Hopkins uses ultralight gear for the sport of it. He also believes the light gear has increased his success.

"I used to fish with 20-pound test, then 17, then 14. Now I'm down to six," he says. "I think I catch more fish. The fish doesn't notice the line."

Light lines and rods also may broadcast more action to the drifting baits. Hopkins has boated channel cats up to 13 pounds with the sensitive, ultralight equipment.

He baits the shad much like you would rig a Texas-style plastic worm. Using a worm sinker and a big worm hook, he starts from the bait's mouth and comes out through the tail.

Positioning his boat perpendicular to the wind, he tosses out two to three sea anchors — collapsible bags that catch water. They act like little yellow parachutes, slowing the boat's drift and keeping it sideways to the wind.

He casts out, lets his bait drift to the bottom, closes the bail of his reel and waits for a bite.

"It's not very complicated," Hopkins says. "That's what's nice about it. Anybody can do it. You can use any boat, even a canoe. And the same technique will work everywhere — Cheney, Lake Afton, Marion, Milford, Toronto — it doesn't matter."

Hopkins and his friends often drift for channel cats well into November, wearing wet suits to protect them from the cold.

"We'll go on morning prairie chicken hunts, then fish all afternoon," he says.

"Late in the year, you might only catch 10 shad, but you'll often catch 10 fish with them."

Because Hopkins catches a lot of catfish, he cooks a lot of catfish and prefers a simple recipe. After skinning the fish, he cuts the meat into small ¼ to ½ inch chunks. He places the chunks in a bowl of complete pancake mix and lets them sit for 20 minutes. He next adds clear soda, such as 7-Up or Mountain Dew, to the pancake mix to form a batter. Then he fries the battered chunks in hot oil for

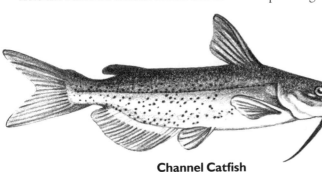

Channel Catfish

about three minutes, until brown.

"It's sweet and good, and it's filling," he says.

Besides late-night drifting, sundown can be a prime time to catch channel catfish, as they rise up points into the shallows of a lake, or move from deep holes to the rapids of a river.

The twilight between day and night is when channel cats are most likely to smash a topwater lure skipped across the surface, or suck up an imitation mosquito placed gently in the eddy behind a rapids-blocking rock.

Bobber fishing with a maggot or worm near shore can be deadly at dusk.

In the middle of the day, plop a bait into a deep, shaded hole in a stream and wait, giving the fish plenty of time to find the bait and think it over. Or cast to the channel of a lake, reel in the slack, set your rod in a holder, then lay back and enjoy the sun, always keeping one eye out for a bouncing rod tip or drifting line.

The more the bait smells, the better; channel cats don't give a whit if it's dead or alive.

Some of the hottest channel catfishing follows right on the heels of a heavy summer rain, especially in rivers and streams above reservoirs. The catfish position themselves at points where runoff waters enter the streams, gorging on nightcrawlers and worms flowing in from the shore.

Nightcrawlers also seem to work best as bait during the channel cats' late-spring spawning season, when the fish head for warm, shallow water to lay eggs in protected areas, such as streambank undercuts.

Big channel cats feed slowly and deliberately, much like large walleye. During the dog days of summer, walleye and channel cats are often caught at the same time by anglers drifting with nightcrawlers over lake mudflats.

One summer afternoon, Elden Bailey was drifting for walleye when he saw his line drift to the side. He leaned his rod tip toward the water and waited until the instant he felt dead weight at the other end. Then he set the hook.

Soon, experience told him it was a channel cat — a big channel cat. Using an ultralight rod and 4-pound test line, he worked the fish carefully for 30 minutes without gaining any ground.

"I almost cut it off," he says. "I told the other guys in the boat, 'I'm sure it's a catfish. I'll just cut it off.' But they said, 'No, you've fought it this long, we might as well see it.

"It took an hour and five minutes to land."

Bailey's channel cat weighed in at 22½ pounds.

It is a world line-test record that still stands.

FLATHEADS

The largest fish ever caught, weighed and recorded in Kansas was an 87.5-pound flathead catfish taken from Pomona Reservoir, on a set line, by Jerry Griffin of Wellsville in 1990.

But any serious flathead fisherman will argue that there are bigger "yellow cats" lurking in the depths of several man-made lakes, particularly Milford, John Redmond, Glen Elder and Fall River Reservoirs.

Most believe that someday, someone is going to haul in a 100-pound flathead.

Mike Cox, a fisheries biologist who serves as Wildlife and Parks information chief, ranks among the believers.

"There is a lot of food available for

Flathead Catfish

those flatheads in the reservoirs and they're less accessible than they used to be in the big, slow-moving rivers," Cox says.

And there used to be catfish in Kansas over 100 pounds — no doubt about it — according to Bill Layher, who wrote a master's thesis about the age, growth rates and feeding habits of flatheads before he became the Wildlife and Parks chief of environmental services.

"I remember one photo from the turn of the century," Layher says. "They were holding two blue cats, caught near Lawrence, that I believe were in excess of 200 pounds. One might have been in excess of 300 pounds."

Blue catfish look much like giant channel cats, with similar blue-gray coloring but no spots. Today, they are infrequent visitors of Kansas waters, occasionally showing up in a tributary of the Missouri

River. The largest caught in modern times came out of the Kansas River and weighed 82 pounds. Channelization of the Missouri likely contributed to the decline of blue catfish.

Flatheads have a mottled yellow-brown coloring, a flat head and a rounded tail. The world record was caught in Texas in 1986 and weighed 98 pounds.

Layher says his father caught a bigger flathead than that, north of Milford, in the 1930s.

"I probably shouldn't say this, but my father was a hand fisherman," Layher says.

Taking catfish by hand — or "noodling" — is now illegal in Kansas.

After finding a huge catfish in a riverside hole, Layher's father and a friend tried to noodle it out of the water.

"They didn't have much luck," Layher says. "So Dad got a rope and a hook and tied the rope to the saddle horn of his horse and dragged the fish out. It weighed in excess of 100 pounds. They put it on display in a stock tank that was probably six foot in diameter and the fish was bent in the tank."

Layher believes catfish of 200 to 300 pounds are gone forever. With large numbers of people fishing for catfish nowadays, he says, potential giants are likely caught before they reach old age.

Giant catfish are "extremely long-lived," according to Layher. A 30-pound flathead might be 16 years old, while a 60-pound catfish is probably in his 30s. Layher wouldn't even guess how old a 300-pound catfish might be.

"I think the catfish populations are essentially being exploited now," he says.

At one time 300 pound cats probably lived in Kansas waters. The official state record flathead weighed 87.5 pounds.

"When white men first settled in the area, there was very little exploitation of fishing. Native Americans relied mostly on buffalo and hadn't really affected the fish population at all."

The largest catfish Layher ever caught in his test nets as a graduate student weighed about 65 pounds. Still, Layher says he "wouldn't be surprised at all if there are flatheads that approach 100 pounds" caught in Kansas reservoirs today.

District fisheries biologist Tom Giffin, who manages Fall River and Toronto Reservoirs, says he would be surprised if there were *not* 100-pound flatheads in Kansas.

"There's lots of food, plenty of water and we've got lots of flathead in the Flint Hills area," Giffin says. "All flathead are hard to catch. The large catfish don't feed as often as the smaller fish. When they do, they're likely to take a three or four-pound fish. People just don't fish with those kind of baits."

If a knowledgeable fisherman spent a week stalking flatheads, dividing his time equally between set lines and rod-and-reel, "he'd have an excellent chance at catching a 50-pounder or better," Giffin says.

Giffin and Layher both are skilled flathead fishermen.

Layher has developed a uniquely sport-

Catfishermen are allowed to bait setlines. Each must have a name tag and be checked regularly.

ing way to catch the big fish. He casts Lazy Ike crankbaits among the rocks below Milford Dam, where big flatheads loiter in protected crevices during the hot months of August and September. As a lure wobbles past its hiding place, a flathead sometimes can't resist sucking it up — and the fight is on.

Unlike most catfish, flathead show a marked preference for live bait. Many fishermen set strong set lines and trotlines across known flathead hot spots, such as bankside spawning areas or below dams on streams.

When setting limb lines, they are careful to tie their ropes to strong branches that are limber enough to bounce with the action of the bait, but thick enough and young enough to withstand the brutal tugging forces of a 50-pound, or larger, cat.

Using large hooks, they bait the lines in evening with live bluegill, sunfish, goldfish or carp. You're likely to catch larger catfish with larger baits — up to three or four pounds — but you'll catch more flatheads using smaller fish.

Often, after setting their lines, flathead fishermen head to another spot to cast out baits with strong poles, which are then placed in shoreline holders. The pole-fishing spot becomes base camp for the night, as they venture out from time to time to see if any nocturnal beasts have taken set line baits.

Experienced flathead fishermen tell lots of stories about finding hooks straightened out and limb-line saplings bent in two. "These fish can be tremendously powerful," Layher says.

A separate group from most rod-and-reel anglers, flathead fishermen develop unique regional techniques from lake to lake and stream to stream. They are usually well known around area bait shops and an inexperienced angler, or one who is new to the area, would be wise to talk to them about their baits and methods.

Don't expect to find out anything about the location of their flathead fishing holes, however. Those you'll have to find on your own.

Section Three

$$H_2O$$

THE GREATEST PUBLIC FISHING opportunities in Kansas are provided by the state's 25 major reservoirs. Many anglers find large bodies of water daunting, but they don't have to be. At any given time of year, game fish will be concentrated in particular areas. By focusing on these high-percentage spots, fishermen can reduce one big lake into a collection of small ponds that are likely to be holding fish. ᗯ Learn as much as you can about the species you hope to catch. How do they move around a lake through the seasons? What time of day are they likely to be most active? How does the weather affect their habits? What lures or baits are most likely to be effective at this time of year? ᗯ The accompanying maps and descriptions detail the key structures and species of each reservoir. We start the tour with a fisherman's dream lake that highlights the various kinds of gamefish hiding, resting, feeding and breeding areas found in Kansas waters.

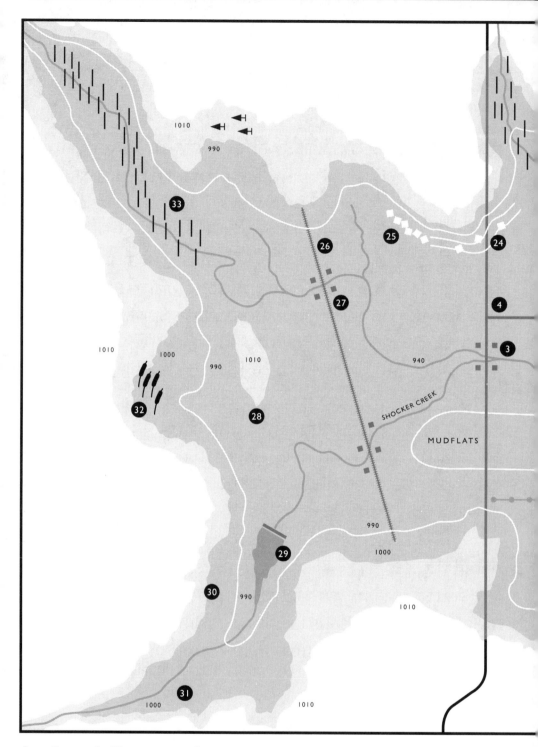

Jayhawk Reservoir

A mythical Kansas impoundment loaded with gamefish hiding places. Use maps, depthfinders and experience to find similar structures in actual lakes.

1. **River channel.** Deep-water highways lined with brush, old stream channels generally provide the most important structure in Kansas lakes. Channel switch-backs are especially productive.

2. **Point near channel.** Fish using channels

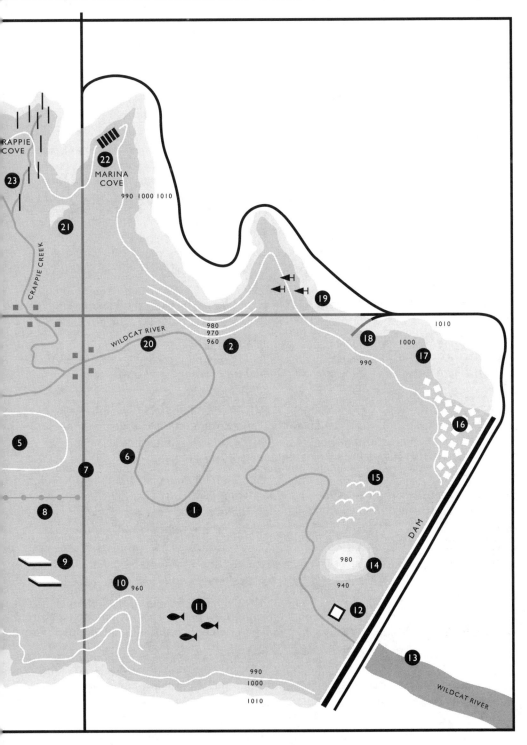

often rise into shallow water to find food. Points offer quick staircases for ambush runs into the shallows. Each contour line indicates a change in depth of 10 feet — a steep dropoff in this case.

3. **Intersections of stream channels** are excellent spots to find gamefish.

4. **Old road intersections** are often lined with timber and brush cover for fish.

5. **Mudflats** are where to look for walleye in May and June, when the fish are rooting through the bottom for mayfly larvae.

Walleye remain on the flats through late summer, as do catfish. When roadbeds and other structures spruce up mudflats, the fishing prospects improve.

6. **Outside bends in channels** often mean holes for walleye, catfish and others.

7. **Old gravel roadbeds** are traveled by game fish, especially walleye.

8. **Old fence line,** with post-rock pilings.

9. **Building foundations,** which may hold walleyes and whites, can be found on old maps or by talking with people who remember the area before it was flooded.

10. **Hidden point.** Gamefish often find prey around points, including those that are invisible from the surface.

11. **Shad schools.** The main forage in Kansas reservoirs, shad lead to crappie, bass, white bass, walleye and stripers. Find schools with depthfinders.

12. **Outlet structure.** Dam and outlet attract fish that prefer rocky structures — smallmouth bass, white bass and crappie.

13. **Spillway.** Below the dam is a good place to find big catfish and March walleye.

14. **A hump** rising from the depths will hold a variety of fish, especially if near other attractors, such as the channel.

15. **Seagulls and terns,** dropping to feed on surfacing schools of shad, reveal the location of white bass and stripers.

16. **Gravel beds** in shallow water that receive moderate wave action become spring walleye spawning grounds.

17. Most maps depict reservoirs at **conservation pool levels,** although depths can fluctuate dramatically. At a pool of 1,000 feet, everything lower than 1,000 feet above sea level will be under water. A spot 940 feet above sea level will be 60 feet deep. That same spot will be 70 feet deep when heavy rains push the lake 10 feet over pool level, or 50 feet deep if the reservoir is drawn down 10 feet below pool. Lake borders shift inward and outward with changing water levels and boating hazards also change. Current lake levels are available from U.S. Army Corps of Engineers offices or area bait shops.

18. Catfish are drawn to the refuse from **boat-ramp area fish cleaning.**

19. **Brushpiles** built with discarded Christmas trees provide great spring crappie cover in shallow coves and at dropoffs.

20. Hot spots offering consistent fishing action usually feature a **combination of attractive structures.** Here we have a point approaching a river channel, a steep dropoff, an outside bend in the channel, an intersection of gravel roads, bridge pilings and a switchback in the river.

21. **Lost Island.** Submerged when lake is filled to pool, underwater islands provide attractive structure for fish. They also become boating hazards when lake levels drop.

22. **Docks** shade crappie, bluegill, catfish and bass.

23. Crappie follow creek channels into **very shallow coves** for spring spawning.

24. **Rocky points** are good spots for walleye, stripers, whites and smallmouth bass

25. **A submerged rock ledge** often hides crappie, smallmouth, walleye and stripers.

26. **Old railroad beds** become gravel roadways for walleye, catfish and other species.

27. **Bridge pilings.**

28. **Island points** often attract fish.

29. **An old watershed pond,** consumed by the reservoir, now provides a deep hole and dam structure for game fish.

30. **Spring spawning grounds.** As the shallow water of incoming creeks warms in early spring, largemouth bass, crappie and catfish head upstream to spawn near bankside structure.

31. White bass travel upstream in schools during spring spawning runs. Channel catfish can be caught in **stream channels** year-round, especially after heavy rains, using worms, crayfish and other baits.

32. **Cattails** offer great crappie fishing during spring spawning season. Also can hold bluegill and largemouth bass.

33. **Flooded timber,** left standing, provides excellent habitat for largemouth bass and crappie.

The State's Reservoirs

 Church

 Recreation area

 School

 Boat ramp

 Airport/landing strip

 Oil well

 Sunken trees

 Marina

 Scouting camp

 Cemetery

 Picnic area

 Sand/gravel pits

 Mudflat area

 Railroad tracks

 Brushpile

 Sunken tires reef

 Dam

Big Hill Reservoir

When the dam on Big Hill Creek was completed in 1981, spring waters flooded over the standing timber, the brushpiles, the man-made fish structures and the valley's ponds. A large bass population, stocked in the ponds shortly before the flood, spread out through the new reservoir and quickly established their domain — just as they were supposed to.

Only trouble was, the bass did even better than fisheries managers had hoped, according to district biologist Lee Dowler.

"The shad never got a chance to start. There apparently were too many bass," Dowler said.

A 12-to-15-inch slot length limit was imposed and anglers were encouraged to remove fish under 12 inches long. They didn't need any encouragement to remove fish over 15 inches, so the upper end of the slot was later raised to 18 inches.

Ever since, Big Hill has been the top largemouth bass reservoir in Kansas.

Dowler shocked up 26 largemouth per hour in his 1990 spring surveys. That was substantially higher than any of the other large reservoirs.

"As a biologist, I wouldn't even think of taking the 18-inch limit off," Dowler says.

"They're throwing a lot of them back. I'm real pleased with the population."

Big Hill features five excellent Corps of Engineers park facilities, which include showers, electrical camping hookups, swimming beaches, nature trails and forested tent camping areas. There are only two boat ramps, however, and the parking lots are typically overflowing on weekends.

Big Hill's flooded timber and brushpiles hide an exceptional crappie population. White bass have not yet become established, and Dowler is glad, as he believes they might compete for food against the crappie.

A fair adult walleye population is present, but natural reproduction has been poor, possibly because of the way water leaves the dam through an uncontrolled pipe. Algae on the spawning beds could also be playing a part in the poor walleye reproduction, Dowler said.

Channel cat shorts were stocked from 1988 through 1991 and a few flatheads roam the reservoir.

A canoe access point lies on Big Hill Creek at the Timber Hill camping area. The creek, which draws its name from a band of Osage Indians that once lived along its banks, offers good spring fishing for crappie and walleye.

BIG HILL

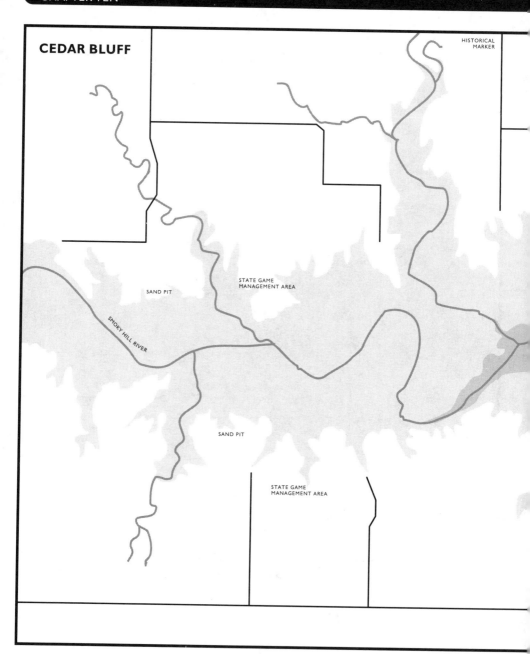

CEDAR BLUFF

HISTORICAL MARKER

STATE GAME MANAGEMENT AREA

SAND PIT

SMOKY HILL RIVER

SAND PIT

STATE GAME MANAGEMENT AREA

Cedar Bluff Reservoir

A remnant of its former self, Cedar Bluff Reservoir has covered about 1,800 surface acres in recent years, compared to its conservation pool of 6,869 acres.

A former federal fish hatchery below the dam is now used as a holding pen for Canada geese and for sharptail grouse that are being reintroduced to northwest Kansas.

Constructed for irrigation in 1951, Cedar Bluff has been reduced in size by irrigators. Central-pivot irrigation systems, in particular, have drawn down the underground aquifer that once discharged slowly into the Smoky Hill basin.

Walleye, white bass, crappie and catfish still populate the lake in reasonable numbers. An 18-inch length limit applies on walleye. Fewer bass are present than in the past, but their numbers sometimes rise

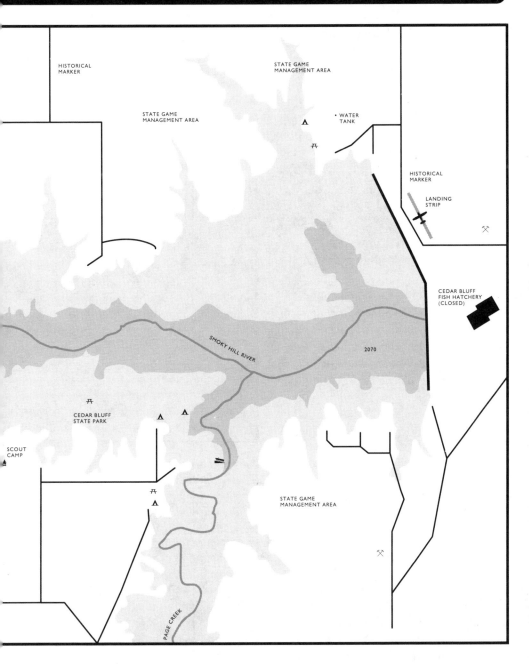

when rare floodwaters raise the lake over the vegetation of adjacent lands, providing additional food and cover.

Smallmouth bass can be taken on occasion off the dam. Largemouth also are caught near the dam and near man-made fish attractors, which are marked. Spotted bass were stocked in Cedar bluff, starting in 1980, and can be taken off the dam and at the edge of dropoffs. White bass fishing is good near shore in springtime and off the dam in early summer. Crappie can be found among the fish-attracting brushpiles in early spring.

Look for channel cats at the west end of the lake and at the line where clear and muddy waters meet. Up-to-date fishing reports are available from the Northwest Region Wildlife and Parks office at (913) 628-8614.

Cheney Reservoir

White bass and channel catfish abound in Cheney Reservoir, crappie populations are strong, and walleye and stripers remain a force although their numbers have declined in recent years.

Cheney was once famous for its spring white bass runs up the North Fork of the Ninnescah River, but siltation appears to have pinched off the inlet enough to reduce the spawning run. Fishing for catfish remains excellent in the river, especially right after a hard rain, using worms and crayfish for bait.

White bass appear to be reproducing well enough at other spawning sights scattered around the lake, said fisheries biologist Gordon Schneider. Located 20 miles west of Wichita, Cheney is one of the state's most popular ice fishing lakes because of its large, aggressive white bass population.

Completed by the Bureau of Reclamation in 1965, Cheney was designed to control floods and conserve water for municipal use in Wichita. Schneider has found a way to turn the lake's proximity to Kansas' largest city into an asset for crappie by asking folks to discard old Christmas trees at the Valley Center Wildlife and Parks office.

Schneider binds together four trees, then dumps them into crappie spawning coves, piling three bundles on top of one another.

"It's simple and it's real effective," Schneider says about his crappie brushpiles. "You don't want the pile to get too big — you want to be able to reach around it and get down into it with lures and bait."

Brushpiles have been dumped in Mud Creek Cove, Fisherman's Cove and elsewhere on the lake. Buoys mark most brushpiles built by Wildlife and Parks as fish areas.

Crappie fishermen should park their boats directly over a brushpile and dangle jigs, or jigs tipped with minnows, down among the branches.

Evergreen piles have been placed under

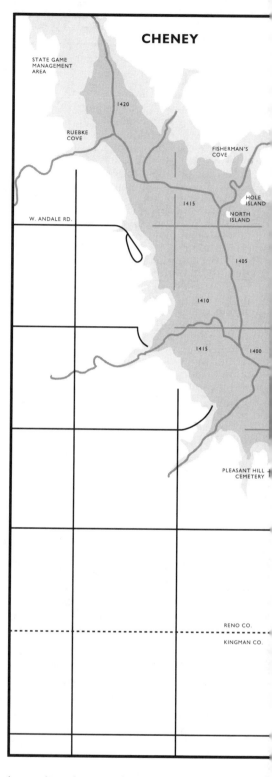

CHENEY

STATE GAME MANAGEMENT AREA

RUEBKE COVE

FISHERMAN'S COVE

W. ANDALE RD.

HOLE ISLAND

NORTH ISLAND

1420

1415

1405

1410

1415

1400

PLEASANT HILL CEMETERY

RENO CO.

KINGMAN CO.

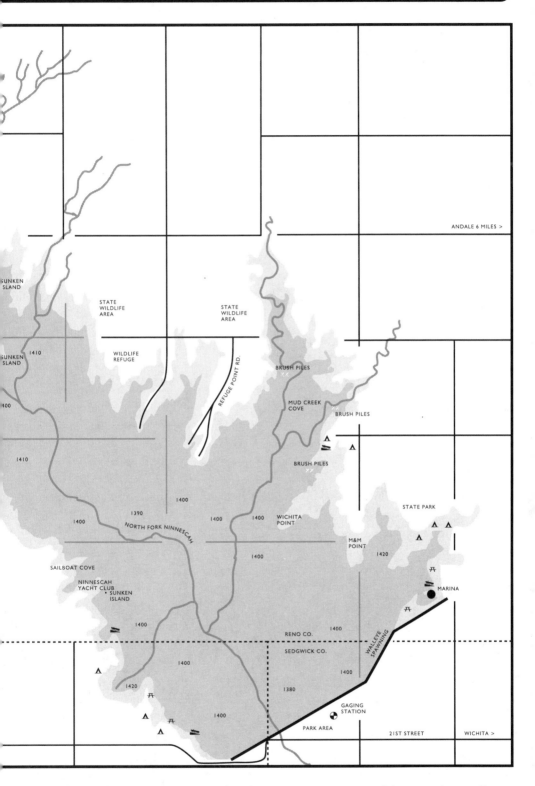

ANDALE 6 MILES >

SUNKEN ISLAND

STATE WILDLIFE AREA

STATE WILDLIFE AREA

SUNKEN ISLAND

1410

WILDLIFE REFUGE

REFUGE POINT RD.

BRUSH PILES

400

MUD CREEK COVE

BRUSH PILES

1410

BRUSH PILES

1400

STATE PARK

1390

NORTH FORK NINNESCAH

1400

1400

1400

WICHITA POINT

1400

M&M POINT

1420

SAILBOAT COVE

NINNESCAH YACHT CLUB
• SUNKEN ISLAND

MARINA

1400

1400

RENO CO.

SEDGWICK CO.

WALLEYE SPAWNING

1400

1400

1420

1400

1380

GAGING STATION

1400

PARK AREA

21ST STREET

WICHITA >

boat slips at the Cheney marina and in the past the general public has been allowed to fish off those docks until about mid-March when the private boat club opens.

Spring crappie fishing can be excellent among cattails in shallow waters, when such areas are available. A high water year can drown out cattails.

Look for walleye early in April around the east end of the dam. Check mudflats for walleye (and catfish) in May and June. An 18-inch length limit applies on walleye.

Cheney's stream channels generally flow right down the center of the lake and most of the reservoir's regular anglers prefer to fish it in a boat.

Some striper fishermen, however, enjoy casting with surf-fishing gear from shore. Using live or cut bait, they cast toward the channels from spots such as Wichita Point, Refuge Island and the beach at the end of W. Andale Road.

Apparently, the hot, dry summer of 1988 proved to be too much for Cheney's big stripers (over 10 pounds). The fish lost their appetites and eventually died in water too warm for them tolerate over a long time, Schneider said.

Because siltation has reduced depth and cover, Cheney may be better suited these days for wipers than for stripers.

Wiper stocking at the lake was delayed, however, by state fisheries officials' concerns that wipers put in the lake would be quickly removed since for years there was no limit on wipers. That changed in 1990 when the Wildlife and Parks Commission approved a daily bag limit of 2 on wipers — same as for stripers. A large number of small wipers were stocked in Cheney in 1990.

At conservation pool, Cheney offers 9,500 surface acres and 67 miles of shoreline. The State Park offers 185 campsites equipped with electricity and there are 20 boat ramp lanes around the lake. A popular lake for boating and sailing, Cheney features a marina on the east shore and a yacht club on the west. The State Park phone number is (316) 542-3664. Lake levels are available from the U.S. Army Corps of Engineers, Tulsa District, at (918) 581-7307.

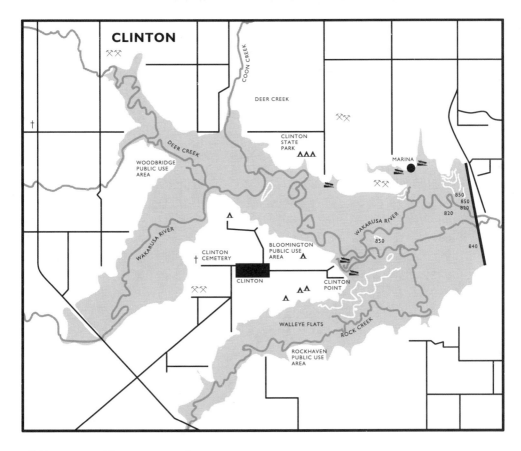

Clinton Reservoir

One of the few lakes in the state featuring cords of flooded timber, Clinton offers exceptional crappie habitat, with very good fishing for largemouth bass, white bass and catfish. Clinton also boasts a re-bounding walleye population.

Both bass and crappie can be found among the trees in the Wakarusa River, Deer Creek and Rock Creek. In midsummer, search for crappie in the river and creek channels.

The Wakarusa has always supported excellent flathead and channel cat populations and Clinton's wooded creek coves provide ample spawning territory for big cats.

Walleye can be found year-round off Clinton Point between the river and Rock Creek. Troll, drift and search for fish clumped around structure as you weave back and forth from the point to the dam.

Clinton Point extends beneath the surface to both channels and halfway to the dam. Walleye move up and down the point throughout the year, with the dam face offering the most action in springtime. Brushpiles along the dropoff and other changes in structure hold fish during the other seasons.

Consistently good fishing spots at Clinton include the first point west of the dam on the north shore, the mudflats scattered among trees in the river arm, and the mudflats north of Rock Creek channel.

At conservation pool, Clinton offers 7,000 surface acres and 72 shoreline miles. A full-service marina operates in the 1,455-acre State Park, which can be reached by calling (913) 842-8562. Lake level and release information is available by calling the Kansas City office of the U.S. Army Corps of Engineers at (816) 374-5241.

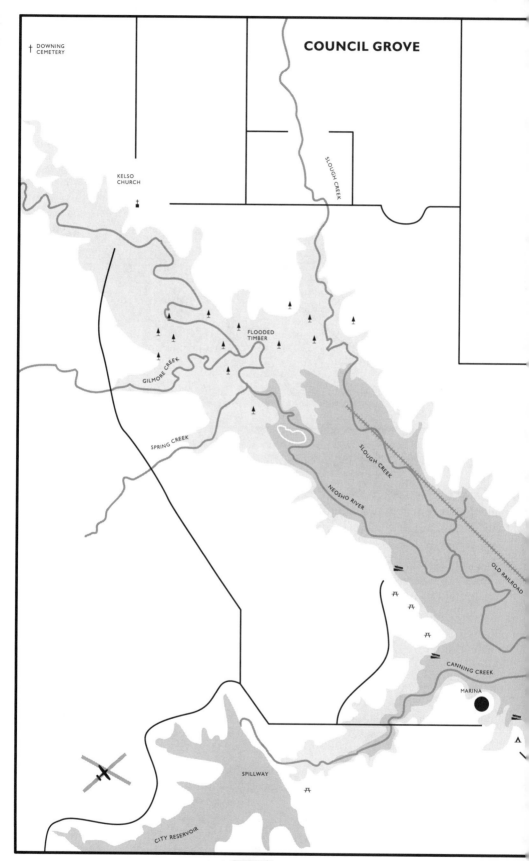

COUNCIL GROVE

† DOWNING CEMETERY

KELSO CHURCH

SLOUGH CREEK

FLOODED TIMBER

GILMORE CREEK

SPRING CREEK

SLOUGH CREEK

NEOSHO RIVER

OLD RAILROAD

CANNING CREEK

MARINA

SPILLWAY

CITY RESERVOIR

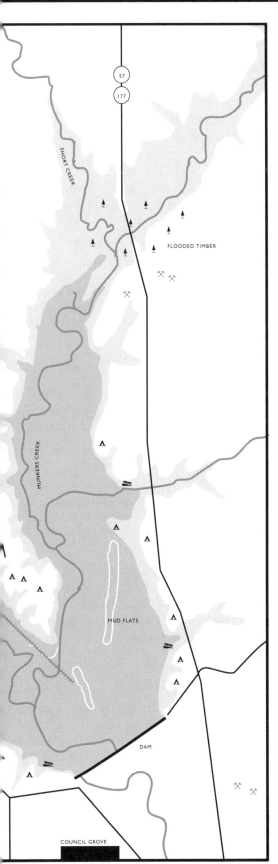

Council Grove Lake

"If you can't find a place to catch fish in this lake, then you're not a fisherman," said Lincoln Bennett, a grizzled angling veteran from Abilene who has been fishing the Neosho River watershed since long before a dam was built at Council Grove.

Completed in 1964, that dam stretches 6,500 feet while rising 96 feet above the Neosho channel. Although a small reservoir of 2,860 acres, Council Grove boasts 37 miles of shoreline.

Most impressive are the confusing mazes of flooded timber at the upper ends of the V-shaped lake. A haunting, rhythmic chorus of birds, frogs and insects sings among the lush backwater jungles, which house mallards, muskrats, wood ducks, Canada geese, great blue herons, woodpeckers, mourning doves and a generous assortment of songbirds.

The wet woods also harbor big crappie, flathead catfish and largemouth bass.

"It reminds me of the swamps in Louisiana," said Robbie Thompson, owner of the lake's marina.

Thompson is an excellent source of information about what is biting where.

Bennett, on the other hand, is an excellent fishermen. His first words to a new acquaintance revealed his fishing savvy — they were designed to cast suspicion on everything he said thereafter.

"You don't have to lie much about your channel cat," he said. "But if you don't lie about your crappie, you've got big problems."

In early May, when crappie head to their shallow spawning areas, Bennett likes to start his evenings with a slow cruise up the Neosho River arm of the reservoir. After he's been seen in the river by all the anglers who ask him about his hot spots, Bennett leaves to fish in another feeder stream.

In recent years, Council Grove has become best known for its crappie fishing. Crappie are the dominant predator species in the lake and often top three pounds in the peak years of their roller-coaster population cycle. Anglers flock to the lake for a chance at "eatin' fish" that thrash like bass.

During the spawning season, Council Grove crappie head to the shallow banks of small coves that line the wedge of land in the center of the V. Especially productive are the coves on the eastern, lee side of the peninsula. Crappie also school in brushy cuts along the stream banks.

At other times of year, crappie roam the lake, much like white bass. While you can find them around brushpiles, as at any reservoir, it often pays at Council Grove to locate shad schools and fish from straight above them.

White bass live in the reservoir as well, and can be found harassing shad around the river channel.

Big largemouth bass hide among the flooded timber at the lake's upper end, which is too treacherous and difficult to navigate for large semi-V bottomed bass boats. You need a flat-bottomed john boat and a paddle for a depthfinder. Even then, chances are good you'll spend some time hung up on a stump.

Flathead catfish of 50 pounds and more are caught up the streams on limblines. Channel catfish, which start spawning just as the crappie stop, can be found in the creeks in late spring and on the flats all summer.

Walleye can be caught drifting or trolling the flats off Richey Cove, but the nearby city lake appears to grow larger walleye. Attracted to beds of gravel along the dam, walleye often get sucked downstream in wet years, when heavy flows of water flush through Council Grove. Biologists have been experimenting in recent years with the walleye-sauger hybrid "saugeye," which they believe may be better able to cope with the reservoir's high flow rates.

Council Grove hides many secret fishing spots. An old-timer like Bennett can point to the water and talk about the old barn foundation or hog pen that lies beneath the surface.

Yet even Bennett's memory pales in comparison to the area's outstanding history. Council Grove is the birthplace of the Santa Fe Trail. It is said to have received its name when the legendary scout Kit Carson held a treaty council with Osage Indian leaders to establish a trail through their territory for wagon trains hauling freight to the southwest.

In a grove of oak trees, where the negotiations took place, Carson cut the words "Council Grove" into a buffalo hide and nailed it to a huge tree under which a treaty was signed in 1825.

For many years, Council Grove was the last outfitting post between the Missouri River and Santa Fe. The stump of the council oak can still be seen on the north side of Main Street in town.

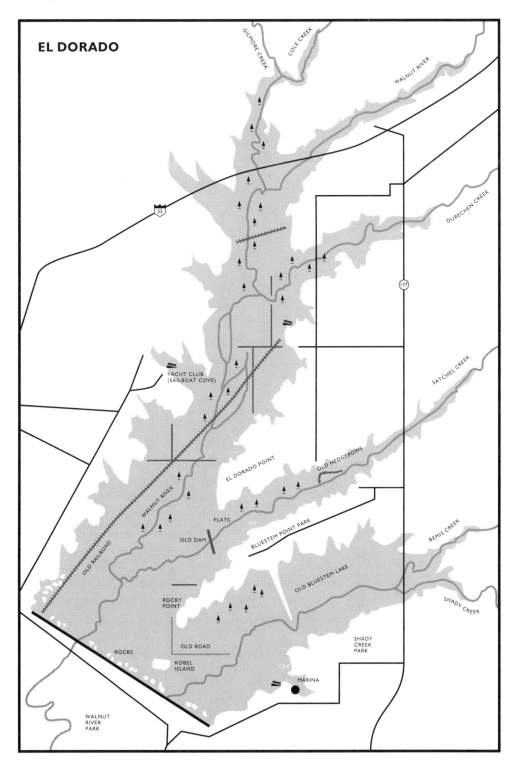

EL DORADO

El Dorado Lake

Designed to be the premier bass fishing lake in Kansas, El Dorado looked like it would reach its potential in 1984, when anglers could pluck a hundred small largemouth from the reservoir in a single afternoon.

Fishing pressure was extraordinary, however, and four years later you could fish hard all day without catching a single bass. The largemouth length limit was raised to 18 inches in 1988, the year fisheries biologist Ron Marteney had once expected to be the lake's peak for productivity.

"That lake was raped," said Steve White, who ran catch-and-release bass tournaments in Kansas for six years. "They aren't doing it anymore because there aren't enough fish in there now."

"In 1984, if you were fishing for food, the easiest thing to catch would have been largemouth bass," Marteney says.

Marteney hopes the longer length limit, combined with increased law enforcement, will foster a rebound in El Dorado's largemouth population. A similar strategy worked wonders at Big Hill Reservoir in southeast Kansas.

Lord knows the habitat exists to support excellent largemouth numbers in El Dorado.

Much of the lake's timber was left standing when the reservoir was flooded. The creek and river channels are loaded with cover.

Crappie habitat also is excellent — and crappie numbers are as well. Crappie can often be found among brushpiles in the flooded timber at the upper end of the lake. Late in the summer, look for them around brush in deeper holes and channels.

Attempts to keep white bass out of the lake failed miserably and the fish now make spring runs up El Dorado's creeks. White bass fishing is good off the dam and points in the lower end of the lake.

El Dorado supports a fine population of hard-fighting smallmouth bass, including some of the largest specimens in the state. Cast crayfish imitations along the dam and rocky points in the reservoir's deep end. When the largemouth length limit was lengthened, the smallmouth limit was maintained at 15 inches, as smallmouth tend to be a shorter, chunkier species.

Walleye numbers crashed in 1986 when rotting vegetation depleted oxygen in the cool depths of the new reservoir. Walleye began a slow but steady recovery in the late '80s and can be found in river and creek channels at the lake's lower end. Look for them especially where points approach the streams and where the channels meet additional structure, such as an old dam or road bed. An 18-inch length limit was applied in 1990.

Channel catfish can be found throughout the lake, especially on the mudflats.

"Channel catfish are booming to the point where they could withstand much higher fishing pressure," Marteney said.

Flathead fishing also is good in the streams.

At conservation pool, El Dorado offers 8,000 surface acres. El Dorado State Park is the largest in the state at 3,800 acres. It offers rough camping as well as 128 sites with sewer, water and electricity, and an additional 352 sites with electrical hookups only. The lake features a large marina and a sailing club.

For state park information and daily fishing updates, call (316) 321-7180. For current lake levels, call the El Dorado Corps of Engineers office at (316) 321-9974.

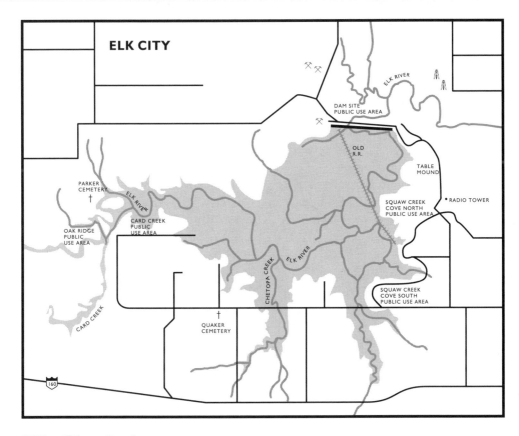

ELK CITY

Elk City Lake

Long the domain of Osage Indians, the Elk River Valley near present-day Independence was eventually settled by veteran Union soldiers from the Civil War.

Home to notorious outlaws, including the Dalton Gang, the area also was where Laura Ingalls Wilder lived briefly as a child and gathered the memories for her famous book "Little House on the Prairie."

A shallow reservoir completed in 1966, Elk City has 4,450 surface acres and 50 miles of shoreline at conservation pool.

Fishing is not exceptional, although the lake supports fair populations of catfish, crappie, white bass and panfish, plus a few largemouth bass. An 18-inch length limit applies on walleye.

Elk City State Park includes 60 campsites with electrical hookups. East of the park is Table Mound, site of an old Osage Indian campsite, where arrowheads and other artifacts are still found from time to time.

A hiking and horse-riding trail snakes through the area's scenic rock bluffs.

State Park information is available by calling (316) 331-6295. Lake level information is available by calling the U.S. Army Corps of Engineers in Tulsa at (913) 581-7307.

Fall River Lake

Tucked in the lovely wooded hills of Greenwood County, Fall River was completed in 1949 and is one of the oldest reservoirs in Kansas.

It also is among the smallest, covering 2,450 surface acres and 40 shoreline miles at conservation pool. Its size is compensated for somewhat by the nearness of its sister lake: Toronto Reservoir. The state parklands at the two reservoirs are managed as one unit.

A shallow but productive lake, Fall River can run fast with high water in springtime, when white bass head north up the river, and its tributary Otter Creek.

The river has long been a popular summer spot for flathead catfish anglers, who fish at night with trot lines and limb lines.

Crappie fishing is excellent along brushy banks during the spring spawn. Look for brushpiles at dropoffs and around the river channel when crappie fishing in summer. Also, jig among shad schools for both crappie and white bass.

Largemouth bass can be found among fallen trees and brush where points reach out toward the river channel, and around brush and undercuts along the stream banks.

Fall River is a beautiful place to camp, hike and canoe, but call ahead to check on water levels, because some spots become inaccessible when the river is running high. Lake level and current release information is available from the local office of the U.S. Army Corps of Engineers at (316) 658-2455. Camping information is available from the State Park at (316) 637-2213.

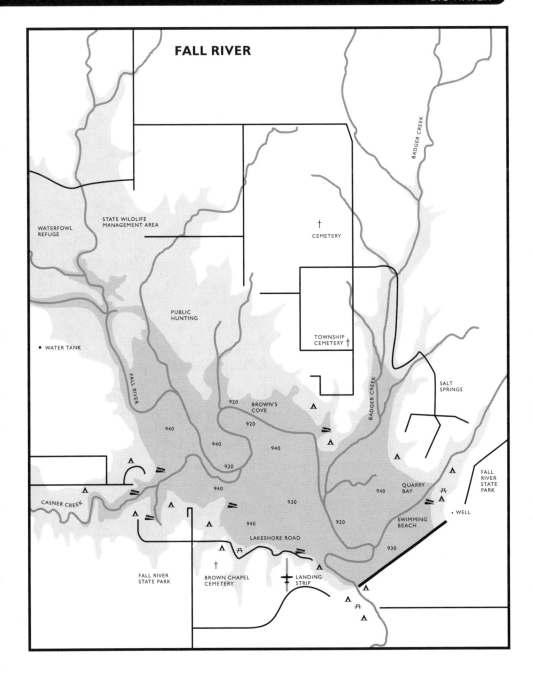

FALL RIVER

BADGER CREEK

WATERFOWL
REFUGE

STATE WILDLIFE
MANAGEMENT AREA

† CEMETERY

PUBLIC
HUNTING

• WATER TANK

FALL RIVER

TOWNSHIP
CEMETERY †

SALT
SPRINGS

920
BROWN'S
COVE

920

940

940

920

940

930

940

BADGER CREEK

QUARRY
BAY

FALL
RIVER
STATE
PARK

• WELL

SWIMMING
BEACH

CASNER CREEK

940

920

930

LAKESHORE ROAD

FALL RIVER
STATE PARK

BROWN CHAPEL
CEMETERY

LANDING
STRIP

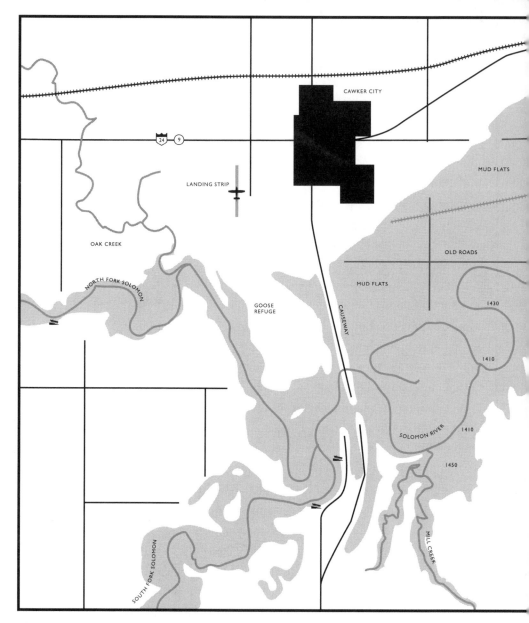

Glen Elder Reservoir

Call it Glen Elder Reservoir or Waconda Lake, the lake with two names in Mitchell County is arguably the most productive gamefish factory in the state.

"This is a big lake, with tons of channel in it," said fisheries biologist Ken McCloskey.

"There's no way to say there's a key spot in Glen Elder. That river channel meets itself coming and going," added champion walleye fisherman Elden Bailey.

Glen Elder received national attention in May, 1988, when 1,000 walleye were caught during a two-day tournament. The success of the competing anglers frightened conservation-minded sportsmen and state resource managers. In 1989, the statewide walleye daily creel limit dropped from eight to five. In 1990, a 15-inch walleye length limit was imposed at the reservoir. The trend toward catch-and-release walleye fishing picked up considerable steam among tournament anglers.

The thousand-walleye weekend came

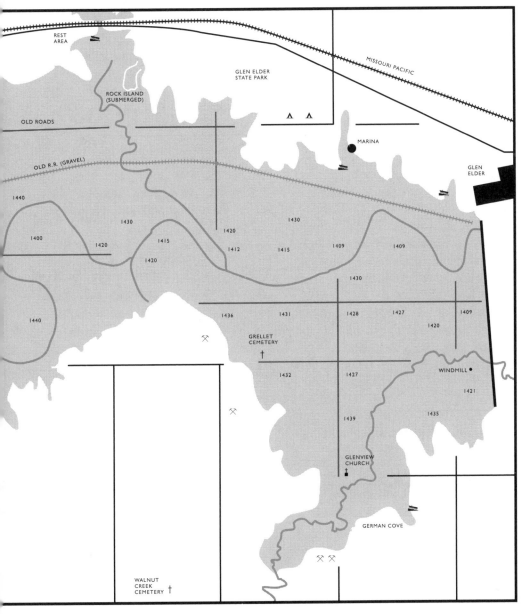

REST
AREA

MISSOURI PACIFIC

GLEN ELDER
STATE PARK

ROCK ISLAND
(SUBMERGED)

OLD ROADS

MARINA

GLEN
ELDER

OLD R.R. (GRAVEL)

1440

1430   1430

1420

1400   1420   1415

1420   1412   1415   1409   1409

1420

1430

1440   1436   1431   1428   1427   1409

1420

GRELLET
CEMETERY
†

1432   1427   WINDMILL •

1421

1439   1435

GLENVIEW
CHURCH

GERMAN COVE

WALNUT
CREEK
CEMETERY †

as fish populations were rising thanks to a year of rest the lake received in 1987. Heavy spring and summer rains that year filled the lake to 15 feet above conservation pool level, making it difficult for anglers to find the boat ramps, let alone the fish. High water also broadened the food and cover supply available to some species. The combination of low fishing pressure and excellent habitat produced quick dividends.

Walleye, stripers and mid-summer crappie follow the creek and river chan-

nels of Glen Elder. Switchbacks, outside bends and spots where points approach the channels are good starting places.

Many old roadbeds line the lake bottom and sunken timber often lies where they intersect.

"Up North, if you read *In-Fisherman*, they always talk about fishing weedbeds," McCloskey says. "We don't have weed beds, we have timber."

Drift fishing the mudflats is especially popular at Glen Elder in May and June. The dam face is an obvious walleye place during the spring spawn. Orange and chartreuse jigs tipped with nightcrawlers are favorite drifting baits.

Glen Elder features sunken islands, rock piles, humps and dropoffs dressed with cedar brushpiles. White bass can often be found surfacing near the causeway, the dam or in shallow coves during early morning and late evening hours. They make solid upstream runs in springtime.

Stripers sometimes surface at Glen Elder in late summer as well, slashing into schools of shad like sharks in a feeding frenzy. More often, stripers can be found suspended in deep river spots or hiding among the shadows of humps and point dropoffs.

Channel catfish are high in number and underutilized, according to McCloskey. Freshwater drum are abundant.

Largemouth bass populations were rising again in the reservoir after a partial draw down in 1988 revived shoreline vegetation. Potentially an excellent bass producer, the lake's largemouth population is vulnerable to overfishing.

Built by the Bureau of Reclamation in 1969, Glen Elder's boat ramps and campgrounds don't compare well with those of reservoirs developed by the Corps of Engineers. Maintenance and trash cleanup outside the State Park area leave much to be desired. At conservation pool, the lake offers 12,586 surface acres and 62 miles of shoreline.

For park information, call (913) 545-3345. For lake levels, call the Kansas City Corps of Engineers office at (816) 374-5241. There are motels within a few hundred yards of the lake's north shore and accurate fishing information can almost always be picked up at Myer's Sporting Goods, in Downs, especially when owner Joe Koops isn't out fishing himself.

302190002364606

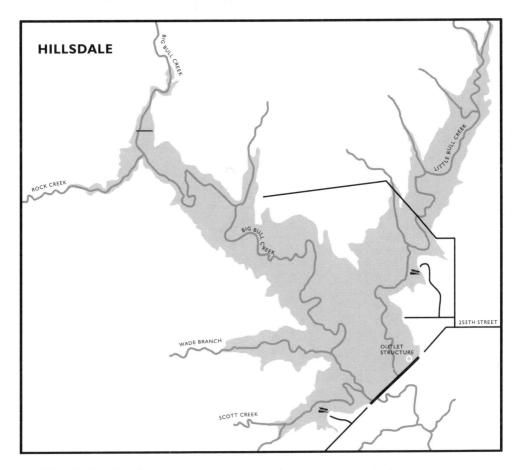

HILLSDALE

BIG BULL CREEK

LITTLE BULL CREEK

ROCK CREEK

BIG BULL CREEK

255TH STREET

WADE BRANCH

OUTLET
STRUCTURE

SCOTT CREEK

Hillsdale Lake

Like Kansas' other three lakes boasting miles of flooded timber — El Dorado, Clinton and Big Hill — Hillsdale is especially popular among largemouth bass and crappie fishermen.

Rich in structure, Hillsdale features winding river and creek channels with lots of switchbacks, old road crossings, dropoffs, humps and points.

In springtime, the intersection of two stream channels often is a good place to start looking for bass. Gradually work the tributary channel into shallower water, following the route bass take to their spawning grounds. If, say, you catch a fish where a finger of land reaches out to the edge of a creek as it enters the main reservoir, then you're likely to find more fish at similar spots elsewhere on the lake.

Dropoffs where river channels brush

close to points can be hot spots in summer, especially if you find a grove of trees standing beneath you. Dangle your lures right among the branches of the old tree canopies, where bass like to linger in the "shade."

Flooded timber and brushpiles provide excellent habitat for crappie as well. Cast jigs to the banks of shallow coves in springtime. Poke around shallow brushpiles in early summer. And search for brush in deeper water around stream channels in mid-summer.

Completed in 1982, Hillsdale is Kansas' youngest reservoir and its facilities were still far from finished in 1990. The lake has been drawn down on several occasions, to build boat ramps and the like, and the high flush rates during draw downs may have hampered development of the lake's walleye populations.

However, lake management was becoming more consistent in the late 1980s and since Hillsdale boasts good walleye structure, numbers should climb in coming years. An 18-inch length limit was imposed in 1990.

State Park facilities were mostly undeveloped at Hillsdale when this book went to press. The lake barely had enough boat ramps to handle the traffic from nearby Kansas City on some weekends.

At conservation pool, the reservoir features 4,580 surface acres and 51 shoreline miles. For fishing and wildlife information, call the Wildlife and Parks Topeka office at (913) 296-2281. For current lake levels, call the Kansas City Corps of Engineers office at (816) 374-5241.

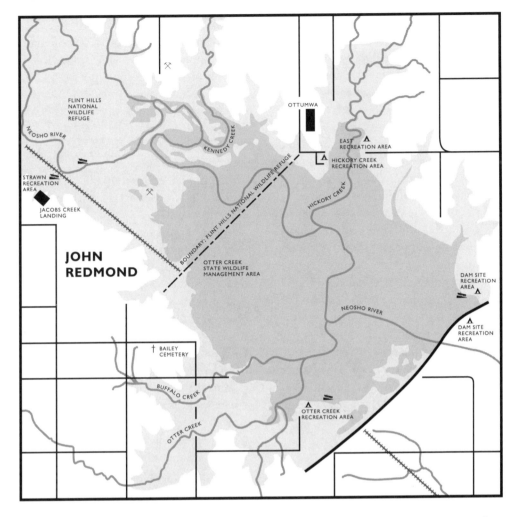

John Redmond Reservoir

John Redmond Reservoir has been described by some as a big mud hole. While this makes it excellent waterfowl habitat and home to the Flint Hills National Wildlife Refuge, it doesn't rank among the state's hottest sportfishing attractions.

Even so, white bass fishing can be excellent up the Neosho River in springtime, and catfish are plentiful. The lake also supports a fair crappie population.

Portions of John Redmond are often closed to fishermen during fall and winter to protect migrating ducks and geese from being pushed away by boat traffic.

Designed primarily for flood control, the reservoir bears the name of the late publisher of the Burlington Daily Republican, who strongly supported dams to control flooding and conserve water in the Neosho River Valley. The fertile valley was flooded 57 times in the 34 years before Congress authorized a dam in 1950. The project was not completed until 1964.

At conservation pool, John Redmond offers 9,400 surface acres of water and 59 shoreline miles. The dam rises 86 feet above the river channel.

Daily lake level information is available from the Tulsa office of the U.S. Army Corps of Engineers at (918) 581-7307.

Kanopolis Lake

Best known for its walleye, wipers and white bass, Kansas' oldest major reservoir also harbors healthy numbers of crappie and channel catfish.

Started in 1940, but delayed by World War II, Kanopolis was finally completed in 1948. Its dam is 15,360 feet long and rises 131 feet above the Smoky Hill River.

The depth of Kanopolis can vary greatly from one year to the next, depending on rainfall. This can make for hazardous boating, but good fishing. When the lake overflows its normal banks after heavy spring rains, new spawning and feeding territories are opened up for gamefish.

"This is probably one of the best early spring lakes in the state. It's smaller and warms up a little faster," said Bob Roberts, an avid fisherman from Salina who considers the 3,400-acre Kanopolis his "home lake."

White bass fishing can be especially hot right after the ice melts. Whites make spawning runs up Bluff Creek and up the river.

At other times of year, white bass can be caught by jigging slab spoons off the bottom under the thick schools of shad that roam Kanopolis. The west shore flats off Boldt Bluff and the dam area are favorite spots to search for white bass.

Kanopolis continued to harbor large wipers, over 10 pounds, from its past, even though few of the hybrids were stocked through the 1980s. A new wiper stocking program began in 1990.

Crappie can be found in the marina cove, around the outlet structure and along the dam.

Loder's Point and other east shore points are good starting spots for walleye fishermen. Walleye also cruise the western mudflats and the dam area.

Nearly all of the lake's species are drawn to three humps at the bottom of the reservoir. The humps appear as a ridge rising into 15 feet of water on depthfinders.

Many tons of silt have washed downstream into Kanopolis over the years, leveling out much of the lake bottom. Old river and creek channels can be difficult to find and even a cut just five feet deep can be significant enough to attract fish.

An area bait shop, the marina and the state park office are good sources of up-to-the-minute fishing information.

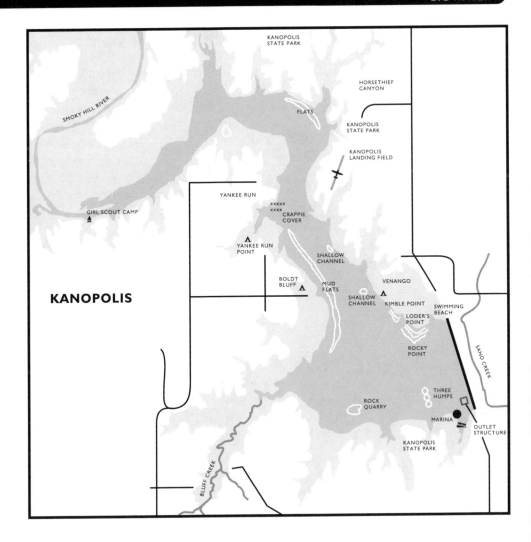

KANOPOLIS

KANOPOLIS
STATE PARK

HORSETHIEF
CANYON

SMOKY HILL RIVER

FLATS

KANOPOLIS
STATE PARK

KANOPOLIS
LANDING FIELD

YANKEE RUN

GIRL SCOUT CAMP

xxxxx
xxxx
CRAPPIE
COVER

YANKEE RUN
POINT

SHALLOW
CHANNEL

BOLDT
BLUFF

MUD
FLATS

VENANGO

SHALLOW
CHANNEL

KIMBLE POINT

SWIMMING
BEACH

LODER'S
POINT

ROCKY
POINT

SAND CREEK

THREE
HUMPS

ROCK
QUARRY

MARINA

OUTLET
STRUCTURE

KANOPOLIS
STATE PARK

BLUFF CREEK

Kirwin Reservoir

In recent years, the pool level at Kirwin has hovered near 1,700 feet above sea level — far below the theoretical conservation pool of 1,728. Maximum depth along the dam is 15 feet.

An extremely low water level in 1990 — down to 1,696 feet — was likely to wipe out many young fish of the year, according to district fisheries biologist Steve Price.

Structure remains excellent in the lake, which is loaded with humps, ridges, breaks and channels. Wipers up to 10 pounds swim in Kirwin, which offers fair fishing for walleye, white bass and crappie.

Kirwin also is home to a national wildlife refuge, which attracts thousands of ducks, geese and cranes every autumn. During one recent autumn, a stray moose even wound up at Kirwin and decided to stay through the following summer.

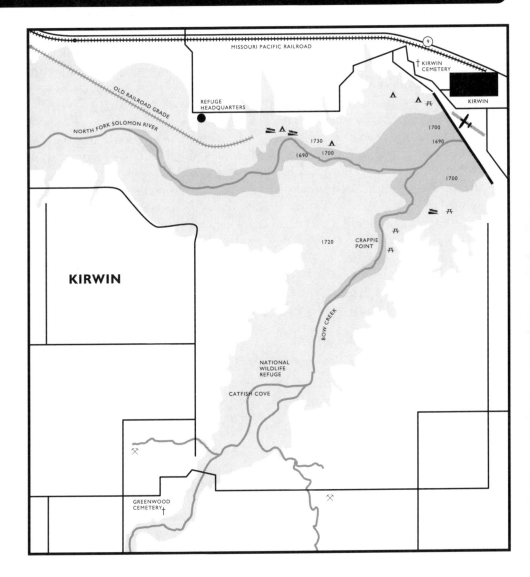

MISSOURI PACIFIC RAILROAD

OLD RAILROAD GRADE

NORTH FORK SOLOMON RIVER

REFUGE HEADQUARTERS

KIRWIN CEMETERY

KIRWIN

9

1700

1690

1700

1730

1690 1700

1720

CRAPPIE POINT

KIRWIN

BOW CREEK

NATIONAL WILDLIFE REFUGE

CATFISH COVE

GREENWOOD CEMETERY

La Cygne Reservoir

The first Kansas reservoir ever developed to cool the waters of a power generating plant, La Cygne's warm waters offer a longer growing season than other lakes in the state. On the other hand, the Kansas City Power and Light Company doesn't like a lot of structure and debris blocking the current of its recycling water supply. As a result, La Cygne does not have the structure to support a huge bass population, although it does contain a respectable number of very large fish.

A Florida strain of largemouth bass was stocked in La Cygne in 1980, in the hope that a state-record fish would later come out of the lake. Not enough bass were stocked, however, to add "more than a drop in the genetic gene pool," said district fisheries biologist Don George.

George has been adding hundreds of large trees, brushpiles and tire reefs to the lake in recent years, providing attractions for largemouth and crappie. Buoys mark most of the underwater structure. Tire reefs lie at the edge of the old stream channel off of the marina cove and along the west shore south of the marina. Brushpiles have been placed on the north shore of the first cove west of the dam, and along the stream channel off the northern border of the 1,000-acre Linn County Park.

The well-maintained park boasts campgrounds, showers, a marina with bait shop, cabins, a swimming pool and even a laundromat. Daily fishing reports are available from the marina at (913) 757-6633.

Public access is restricted from the dam, the spillway and the eastern shore of the reservoir's lower end. Boat access is also restricted from the eastern shore site where water is sucked into the plant.

The plant outlet, at the north end of the lake, is a hot spot for white bass fishermen. A remnant striper population exists but is fading fast, because large stripers can't withstand the lake's high temperatures, which sometimes top 90 degrees at the surface.

Wipers and walleye have been stocked in recent years and should begin to provide good fishing opportunities sometime in the early 1990s. There is an 18-inch length limit on walleyes and a 15-inch limit on bass.

La Cygne supports an abundant channel catfish population, George says, and crappie fishing has been improving around the added structure.

La Cygne covers 2,600 surface acres, with a maximum depth of 40 feet and an average depth of 15 feet. It lies five miles east of the town of La Cygne and 55 miles south of Kansas City.

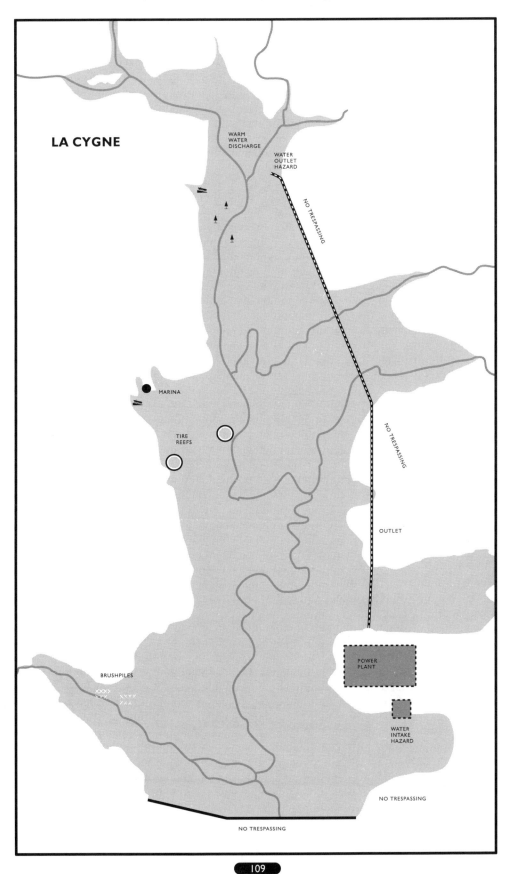

LA CYGNE

WARM WATER DISCHARGE

WATER OUTLET HAZARD

NO TRESPASSING

MARINA

TIRE REEFS

NO TRESPASSING

OUTLET

BRUSHPILES

POWER PLANT

WATER INTAKE HAZARD

NO TRESPASSING

NO TRESPASSING

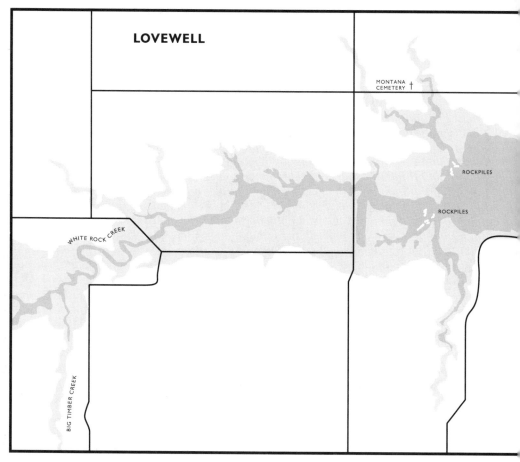

LOVEWELL

MONTANA
CEMETERY

ROCKPILES

ROCKPILES

WHITE ROCK CREEK

BIG TIMBER CREEK

Lovewell Reservoir

A shallow lake, Lovewell features both an inlet and outlet structure at the dam, which is unique in Kansas. The inlet, at the north end of the dam, can be an excellent spot to find spring walleye.

While Lovewell is best known for its walleye, the population crashed in the 1980s, possible because of intense fishing pressure. An experimental 18-inch walleye length limit was imposed in 1988 and stocking was stepped up. The walleye rebounded quickly.

Topographic maps of Lovewell do not show river and creek channels. Segments of channel can be located with sonar, however.

The lake's deepest area is 30 to 35 feet at the dam, and that's where to find walleye when the ice leaves in April. However, the dam may be off-limits to anglers during spawning season if Wildlife and Parks biologists are netting for brood stock there.

Away from the dam, maximum depths reach only 20 feet. Walleye can be found around rock piles in the shallow western end. Walleye also hide among a pile of brush and tires near Oak Hill Recreation

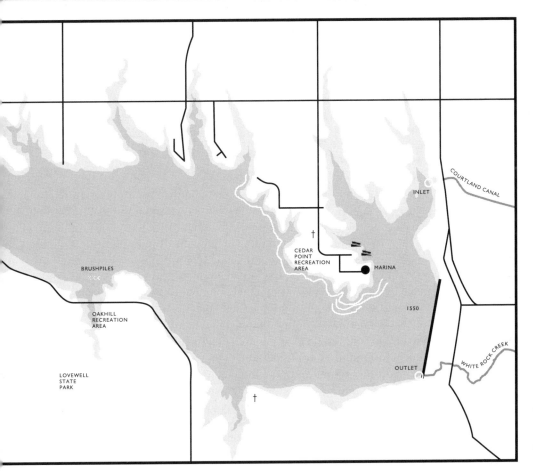

Area about halfway down the lake's south shore.

Cedar Point, which faces the dam, is always worth a check.

Made up mostly of mudflats, Lovewell also offers fine fishing for channel cats. A Bureau of Reclamation project, Lovewell boasts a marina and a 1,126-acre State Park. For daily updates, call the park office at (913) 753-4305 or the regional fisheries biologist at (913) 454-6315.

Marion Reservoir

One of the state's top white bass factories, Marion also harbors healthy numbers of crappie, walleye and catfish, with some spotted bass and wipers tossed in for good measure.

Large numbers of big white bass roam around Marion in search of shad. When you can't spot surfacing shad schools, check the stream channels and face of the dam. Marion offers some of the state's finest ice fishing for white bass, crappie, walleye and catfish, when winter provides enough chill to form thick, safe ice.

The Cottonwood River channel hugs the west shore of the upper half of Marion Reservoir, where constantly changing depths range from 4 to 20 feet. Loaded with humps, dropoffs and mudflats, it is an excellent area for trolling and drifting after walleye.

Spring crappie fishing can be excellent in coves up the stream arms of the lake and among cattails in the lake shallows.

Spotted bass are native to the river, as are channel and flathead catfish. The Santa Fe Trail crossed the Cottonwood just above the reservoir, at Durham.

When full but not flooded, Marion provides 6,200 surface acres and 60 shoreline miles. A 400-acre park run by the U.S. Army Corps of Engineers includes 50 campsites with electricity and can be reached by calling (316) 382-2101. Corps personnel know current lake level and release rate, and can often provide an up-to-date fishing report.

Nearby Marion City Lake is very pretty and offers decent fishing, for a small fee. The lake harbors crappie, walleye, largemouth bass and nice-sized spotted bass.

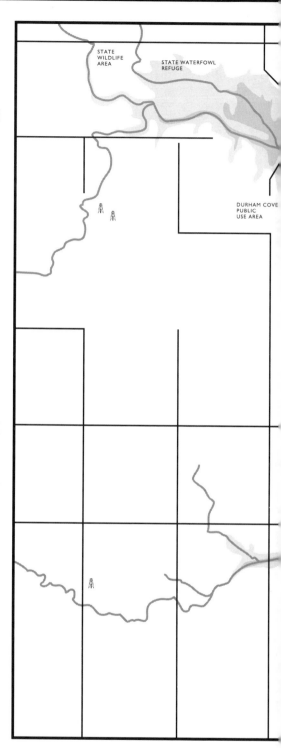

STATE WILDLIFE AREA

STATE WATERFOWL REFUGE

DURHAM COVE PUBLIC USE AREA

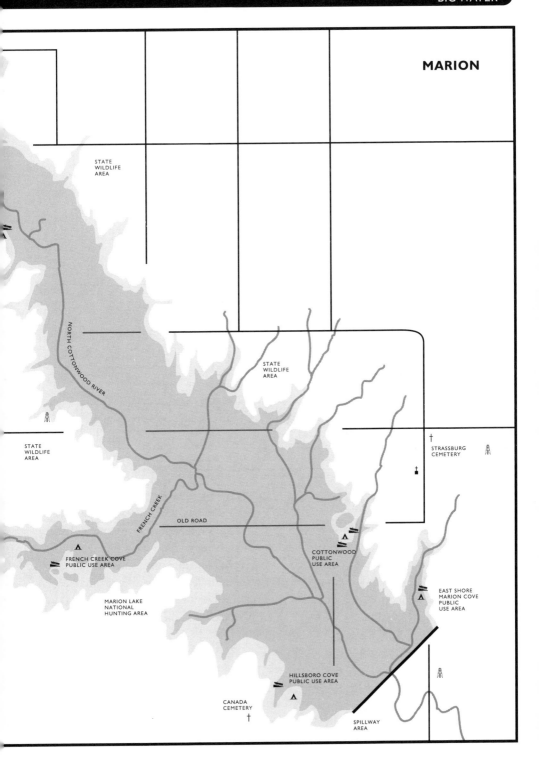

MARION

STATE
WILDLIFE
AREA

NORTH COTTONWOOD RIVER

STATE
WILDLIFE
AREA

STATE
WILDLIFE
AREA

STRASSBURG
CEMETERY

FRENCH CREEK

OLD ROAD

FRENCH CREEK COVE
PUBLIC USE AREA

COTTONWOOD
PUBLIC
USE AREA

EAST SHORE
MARION COVE
PUBLIC
USE AREA

MARION LAKE
NATIONAL
HUNTING AREA

HILLSBORO COVE
PUBLIC USE AREA

CANADA
CEMETERY

SPILLWAY
AREA

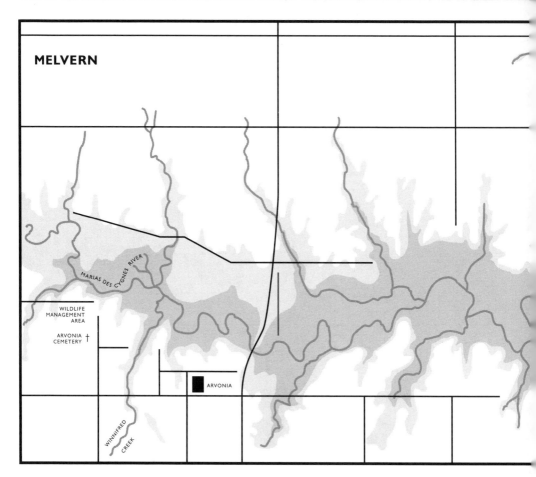

MELVERN

MARIAS DES CYGNES RIVER

WILDLIFE
MANAGEMENT
AREA

ARVONIA
CEMETERY

ARVONIA

WINNIFRED CREEK

Melvern Reservoir

For years, Melvern Reservoir was one of Kansas' most consistent producers of walleye. That began to change in the 1980s as the state reduced walleye stocking at Melvern. Then, in the summer of 1990, a strange surfacing of bottom-dwelling invertebrates overwhelmed the lake, killing many catfish and forcing officials to close the lake to anglers.

The outbreak may have forced state fisheries officials to take a good look at the lake, which might prove beneficial in the long run, suggests angler Elden Bailey, a long-time fan of Melvern's.

"If they stocked it again, it would be a good walleye lake. I'm sure they will now," Bailey said after Melvern was closed.

Even after walleye stocking declined, Melvern continued to yield its share of seven-pounders and up. An 18-inch length limit applies. Fishing for crappie and white bass has continued to be strong, and fishing for channel and flathead catfish was excellent before the invasion of the muck dwellers.

In springtime, crappie head for the many coves lining the south shore of the lake, as well as Turkey Creek and the two State Park coves on the north shore.

White bass spawn up the river and

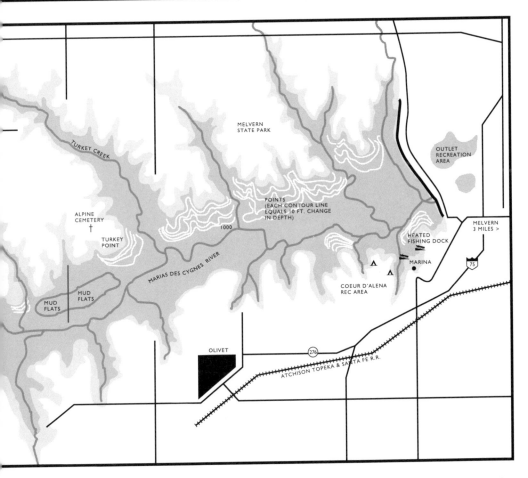

creeks and tend later to cluster off points in the lower third of the lake, toward the dam. The end of Turkey Point and mouth of Marion Cove are favorite white bass hangouts.

Largemouth bass head up the creeks to spawn, and especially favor those on the south and west ends of the lake.

The points and mud flats between Turkey Point and the dam, on the north shore, are probably the best overall place to catch walleye and catfish. The Turkey Creek channel is deep and traveled by many species, as is the Marais des Cygnes.

Melvern boasts some of the finest camping and boat ramp facilities in Kan-

sas. Its 18 boat-ramp lanes are second only to Cheney Lake, which receives much greater fishing pressure.

Melvern has 200 campsites with electrical hookups and 1,785 acres of state park land. A heated fishing dock near the marina offers good fishing from shore during the winter months. State Park information is available at (913) 528-4900. Lake levels and release rates can be discovered by calling the Tulsa office of the Corps of Engineers at (918) 581-7307.

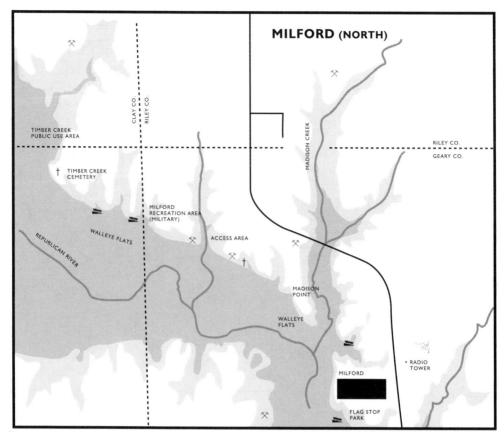

Milford Lake

The State's largest lake, Milford supports a great variety of fish, although it probably is best known for crappie and walleye.

White bass head up the Republican River in early spring to spawn, while crappie seek out the river's coves. Spawning crappie also can be found in the creeks, Quarry Cove, and marina area.

Walleye congregate along the dam face in springtime, of course. Other top walleye hangouts include the mudflats west of Military Cove, Madison Point and the flats between the point and Madison Creek, Farnum Point and the flats south of Farnum Creek, Quarry Cove and a portion of old roadbed between Quarry Cove and School Creek.

The north and south points of School Creek are productive walleye spots, as are Curtis Creek and a pair of humps, or islands, near the dam.

Milford boasts both smallmouth and largemouth bass, with largemouth heading to shallow, brushy streamside breeding areas each spring while smallmouth stick mostly to the lower third of the lake, along the dam and nearby rocky points.

Milford supports excellent populations of both flathead and channel catfish, with the spillway below the dam providing top-notch flathead fishing when water is high.

Milford State Fish Hatchery and Conservation Education Center lie below the dam on the outlet ponds. Built as a state-of-the-art warm water gamefish hatchery in the early 1980s, the hatchery never has lived up to its promise. Marginal water quality has hampered attempts to produce largemouth and smallmouth bass shorts, wipers, spotted bass and even channel catfish, which have been plagued by gill diseases in hatchery raceways.

The hatchery has done a fairly good

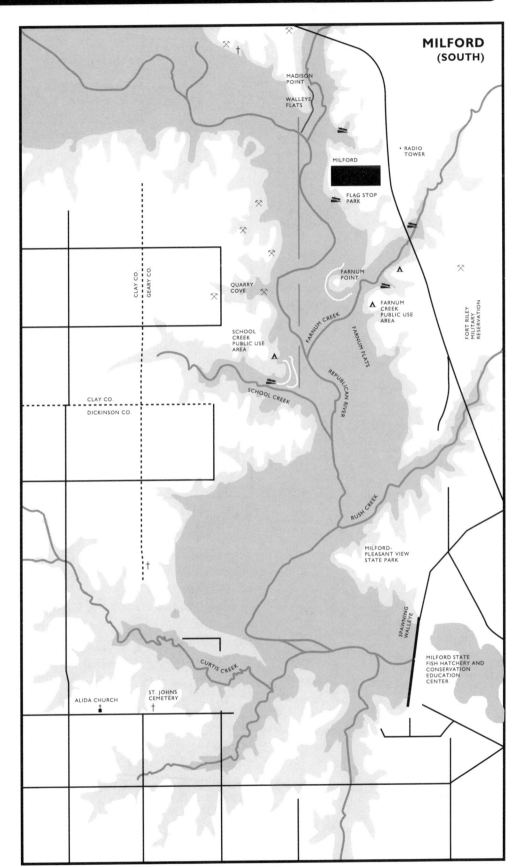

MILFORD
(SOUTH)

MADISON
POINT

WALLEYE
FLATS

MILFORD

• RADIO
TOWER

FLAG STOP
PARK

FARNUM
POINT

FARNUM
CREEK
PUBLIC USE
AREA

CLAY CO.
GEARY CO.

QUARRY
COVE

SCHOOL
CREEK
PUBLIC USE
AREA

FARNUM CREEK

FARNUM FLATS

FORT RILEY MILITARY RESERVATION

SCHOOL CREEK

REPUBLICAN RIVER

CLAY CO.
DICKINSON CO.

RUSH CREEK

MILFORD-
PLEASANT VIEW
STATE PARK

SPAWNING WALLEYE

MILFORD STATE
FISH HATCHERY AND
CONSERVATION
EDUCATION
CENTER

CURTIS CREEK

ALIDA CHURCH

ST. JOHNS
CEMETERY

job of hatching walleye fry, however, and Milford Reservoir benefits directly as a result.

Many amenities are available in the area, including a 1,084-acre State Park with 86 sites wired for electricity and another 32 hooked up for sewer, water and electric.

You can reach the State Park by phoning (913) 238-3014. For up-to-date lake level information, contact the Kansas City office of the Corps of Engineers at (816) 374-5241.

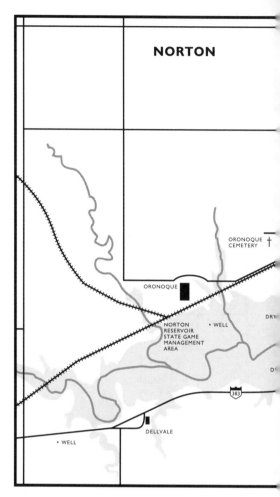

Norton (Sebelius) Lake

Wipers and largemouth bass add excitement to Norton Lake, a.k.a. Keith Sebelius Reservoir.

One of the first lakes in Kansas stocked with wipers back in 1977, Norton likely was harboring some that tipped the scales at 15 pounds or more by 1990, according to fisheries biologist Steve Price. About half of Norton's wiper population topped 10 pounds, he said.

Large wipers can be quite shy and challenging to catch. Sometimes they hug stumps, brushpiles and humps in the deep end of Norton, other times they roam throughout the lake.

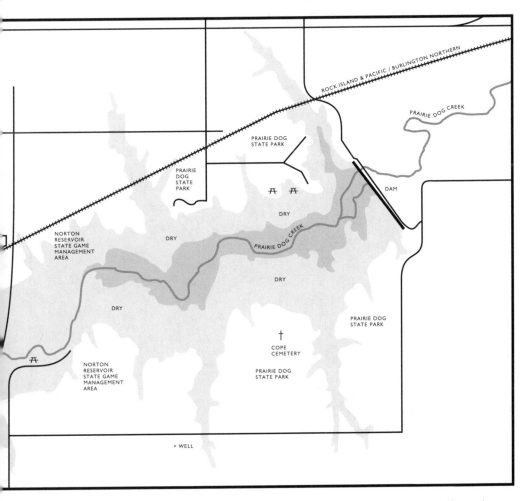

"They're a moving son-of-a-gun," Price said.

Whenever water levels are high in the river, the wipers migrate upstream.

Wipers in Norton are protected by a 12-inch length limit, as well as the state-wide creel limit of just two fish per day.

Norton boasts plenty of stumps, brush and cattails for largemouth bass, which are protected by a 15-inch length limit. Price strongly encourages catch-and-release fishing for largemouth at Norton, where the biggest bass in recent years have weighed about seven pounds.

Crappie abound in Norton and many very small crappie are caught for every keeper tossed in the livewell.

Walleye reproduced naturally in the lake for the first time in the spring of 1990, after the addition of new man-made gravel spawning beds. The lake's old walleye spawning grounds were left high and dry by declining water levels. Designed, like most western reservoirs, for irrigation, Norton's average pool level in recent years has been 2,283 feet above sea level.

Channel catfish numbers were high in 1990 but tend to drop quickly after a few dry springs in a row, Price says.

For updated information about fish populations at Norton, call the Wildlife and Parks office in Webster at (913) 425-6775.

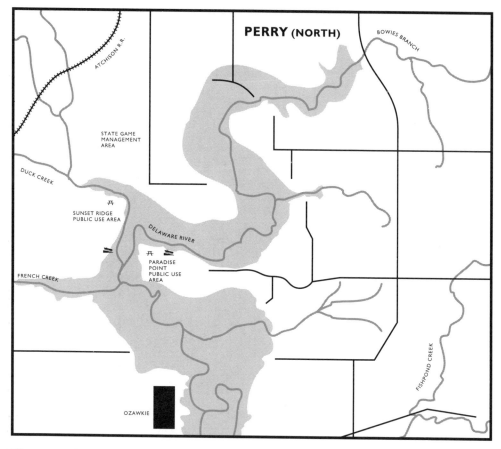

Perry Reservoir

A lovely lake in the Delaware River Valley of northeast Kansas, Perry Reservoir lies just 48 miles west of Kansas City.

Perry offers consistently good spring crappie fishing in coves up the Delaware, Rock Creek and Slough Creek arms of the lake. The Little Slough cove also offers good crappie fishing, as do the points on the southwest shore, near the dam.

While Perry no longer is known for harboring large numbers of walleye, anglers catch a few trophy walleye year in, year out.

Walleye fishermen should pay close attention to the river and creek channels, the Devil's Gap area, the flats north of Slough Creek, and Cemetery Point in Rock Creek. Spring walleye can be found along the dam.

Perry can be an excellent lake for channel catfish.

One of the finest hiking trails in Kansas follows the eastern shore of Perry from the tip of Little Slough Cove in the north to the Devil's Gap hollow in the south. The trail features several access sites. Hikers starting, say, at Devil's Gap can head to end points from 2.7 to 14.5 miles away.

At conservation pool, Perry offers 12,600 surface acres and 160 miles of shoreline. It features excellent camping and boat ramp facilities and a 1,679-acre State Park. Wildlife and Parks personnel can be reached at (913) 289-3449, while daily lake levels and releases are available from the Kansas City Corps of Engineers office at (816) 374-5241.

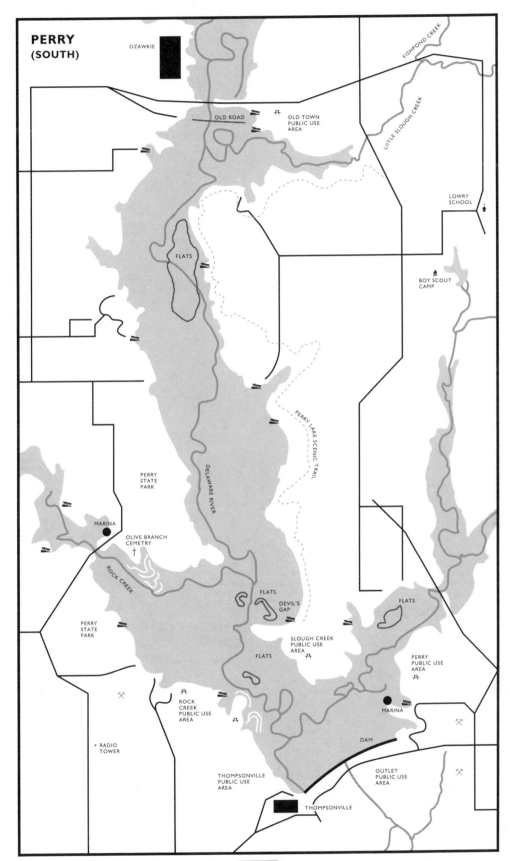

PERRY
(SOUTH)

OZAWKIE

FISHPOND CREEK

LITTLE SLOUGH CREEK

OLD ROAD

OLD TOWN
PUBLIC USE
AREA

LOWRY
SCHOOL

FLATS

BOY SCOUT
CAMP

PERRY LAKE SCENIC TRAIL

DELAWARE RIVER

PERRY
STATE
PARK

MARINA

OLIVE BRANCH
CEMETERY

ROCK CREEK

FLATS

DEVIL'S
GAP

FLATS

PERRY
STATE
PARK

SLOUGH CREEK
PUBLIC USE
AREA

PERRY
PUBLIC USE
AREA

FLATS

MARINA

ROCK
CREEK
PUBLIC USE
AREA

RADIO
TOWER

DAM

THOMPSONVILLE
PUBLIC USE
AREA

OUTLET
PUBLIC USE
AREA

THOMPSONVILLE

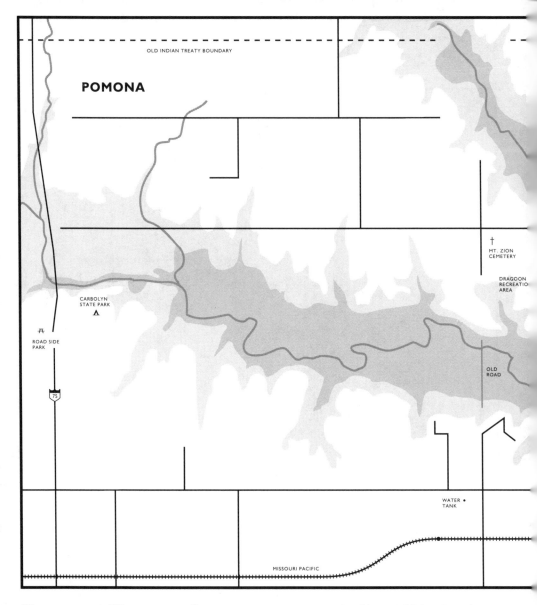

OLD INDIAN TREATY BOUNDARY

POMONA

† MT. ZION CEMETERY

DRAGOON RECREATION AREA

CARBOLYN STATE PARK

ROAD SIDE PARK

75

OLD ROAD

WATER • TANK

MISSOURI PACIFIC

Pomona Reservoir

The largest fish ever caught, weighed and registered in Kansas came out of Pomona Reservoir in 1990: an 87.5-pound flathead catfish.

Pomona also offers good fishing for crappie, channel cats and white bass, in addition to limited fishing for largemouth bass and walleye. Wipers will be a fish of Pomona's future.

Crappie head to the coves and timber along Wolf Creek during spring spawning season. Bass also like Wolf Creek early in the year, as well as Dragoon and Hundred-and-Ten-Mile Creeks.

As waters warm, patrol the stream channels for crappie, catfish and bass, especially in locations where the channels twist to form more edge habitat.

Walleye numbers are limited, in part, by Pomona's high springtime flow rates, which flush spawning fish and their eggs off the face of the dam and out of the reservoir. However, the lake always manages to hang onto a fair number of large survi-

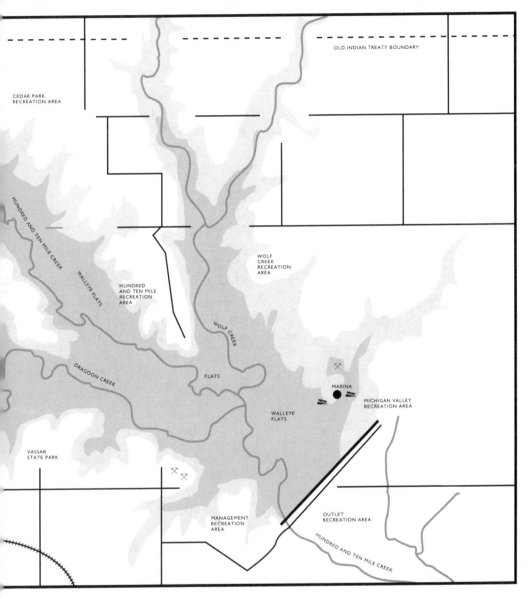

CEDAR PARK
RECREATION AREA

OLD INDIAN TREATY BOUNDARY

HUNDRED AND TEN MILE CREEK

WALLEYE FLATS

HUNDRED
AND TEN MILE
RECREATION
AREA

WOLF
CREEK
RECREATION
AREA

WOLF CREEK

DRAGOON CREEK

FLATS

MARINA

MICHIGAN VALLEY
RECREATION AREA

WALLEYE
FLATS

VASSAR
STATE PARK

MANAGEMENT
RECREATION
AREA

OUTLET
RECREATION AREA

HUNDRED AND TEN MILE CREEK

vors. Search for them on mudflats between the dam and Wolf Creek, on flats
flanking the north side of Hundred-and-
Ten, and along the Dragoon channel
edges.

White bass head up the Dragoon on
their spring spawning runs, with good
fishing found as far west as the Highway
75 bridge.

At conservation pool, Pomona offers
4,000 surface acres and 52 shoreline miles.
Pomona's full-service marina offers boat
rentals and the 490-acre State Park includes 94 campsites with electrical hookups and 37 with electricity, water and
sewer. A summer stock playhouse and golf
and tennis facilities are nearby.

Pomona State Park phone is (913) 828-
4933. For lake level and release rate, call
the Kansas City office of the U.S. Army
Corps of Engineers at (816) 374-5241. Updates on the fishery area available from the
Wildlife and Parks Topeka office, (913)
275-6740.

Toronto Reservoir

Completed in 1960, Toronto Reservoir is part of a massive flood-control system aimed at limiting damage from high water to points hundreds of miles downstream in the Arkansas and Mississippi River Valleys.

Known best for big white bass and catfish, Toronto produced Kansas' first world record: a 5-pound, 4 ounce white bass, back in 1966.

Whites run up the Verdigris in early spring and chase shad schools around the 2,800-acre reservoir the rest of the year.

Channel cats are abundant in Toronto and many flathead fishermen believe the reservoir is one of the most likely lakes in the state to harbor a 100-pound flathead.

Toronto supports some walleye and largemouth bass, as well as an abundant sunfish population.

Limestone outcroppings topped with black oaks overlook the reservoir, which features 1,075-acres of state park land. For more information about lake levels and releases, call the local Corps of Engineers office at (316) 658-2455. For Toronto/Fall River State Park information, call (316) 637-2213.

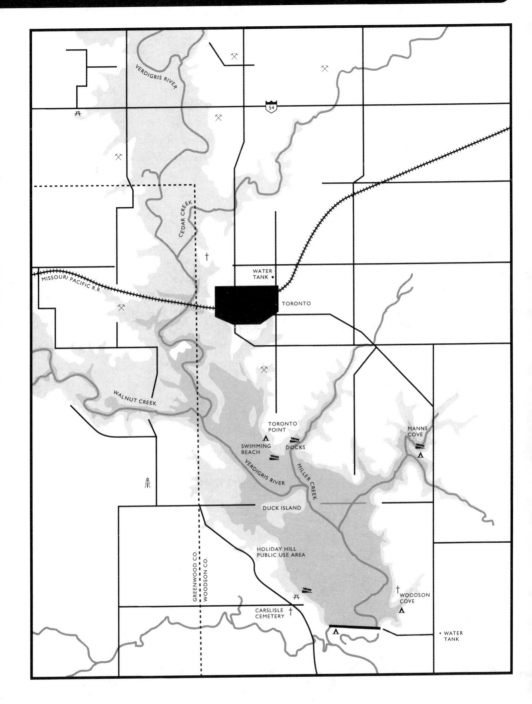

VERDIGRIS RIVER

54

CEDAR CREEK

WATER
TANK

MISSOURI PACIFIC R.R.

TORONTO

WALNUT CREEK

TORONTO
POINT

MANNS
COVE

SWIMMING
BEACH

DOCKS

VERDIGRIS RIVER

MILLER CREEK

DUCK ISLAND

HOLIDAY HILL
PUBLIC USE AREA

GREENWOOD CO.
WOODSON CO.

WOODSON
COVE

CARSLISLE
CEMETERY

WATER
TANK

Tuttle Creek Lake

A cyclic lake dominated by a cyclic species, Tuttle Creek's stock among anglers rises and falls with its crappie population.

Here, as at other reservoirs, crappie congregate along the brushy banks of shallow coves during spring spawning season. But in years when the fish are large in size and number, you can find them by accident almost anywhere.

In 1989, for instance, a group of Kansas outdoor writers converged on Tuttle. While waiting in a just-launched boat for his partner to return from parking the truck, Jim Ramberg of Topeka idly cast a jig toward shore and bounced it back slowly across the bottom.

A fish hit it — his first nice crappie of the day. Hours passed before the boat-ramp action ceased.

Meanwhile, across the lake, nature was calling Wildlife and Parks information officer Mark Shoup. While waiting for Shoup to return from the outhouse, *Kansas Wildlife* magazine editor Mike Miller cast a jig toward the bank and bounced it back slowly across the bottom.

A crappie hit it, and soon Miller's boat was surrounded buy other anglers who had blown the hot spot earlier in the day after launching from the ramp. Only keeping the largest slab-sides, their livewells quickly filled up.

In both cases, stream channels hugged the cove banks near the boat ramps. When a quick cold front put a temporary damper on spawning activity, the crappie grouped back up in schools and gravitated toward areas featuring structure and depth near the mouths of coves.

In addition to finding crappie in coves during spawning season — and at the mouths of coves just before the spawn — look for them at Tuttle Creek among cattail stands in springtime and among flooded trees most anytime of year. If you find a stand of flooded trees in deep water, along a channel, you've found a likely crappie hideout. You may lose a lot of chartreuse jigs while dangling them among the branches, but it will be worth it if the crappie are biting.

Tuttle looks and often behaves more like a wide river than a lake. One mile wide and 17 miles long, it is the second largest reservoir in Kansas at conservation pool, boasting 15,800 surface acres and 112 miles of shoreline.

When spring moisture is high, Tuttle becomes very muddy and water flushes rapidly through the reservoir. Often the best spring walleye fishing can be found not on the face of the dam, but below it, in the outlet channel, as spawning walleye are flushed off the rocks and out of the lake.

With long mudflats, Tuttle supports healthy numbers of channel and flathead catfish. There are plenty of pretty places to fish from shore at Tuttle Creek, which is surrounded by rolling, wooded hills. Rowing crews from nearby Kansas State University add to the beauty of the scenery as they skim their shells gracefully across calm waters.

Some nice largemouth come out of Tuttle Creek's timber and brushy shallows from time to time — they are often caught incidentally by anglers seeking crappie or catfish.

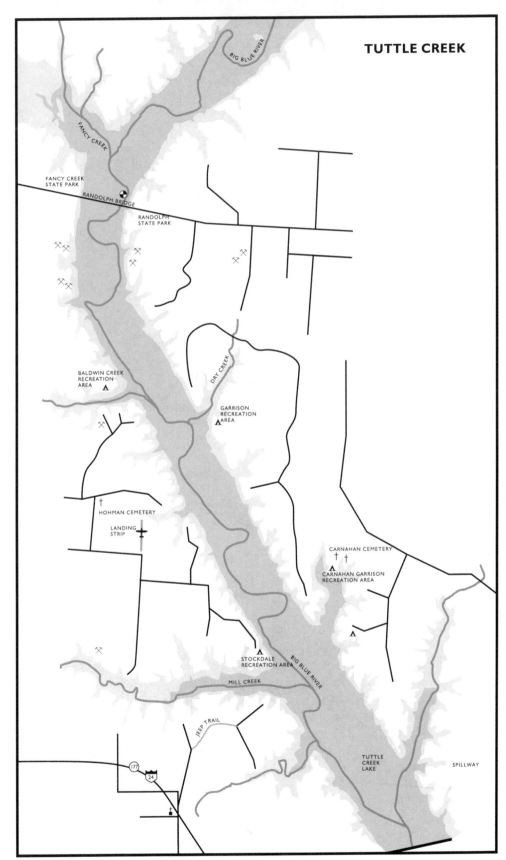

TUTTLE CREEK

BIG BLUE RIVER

FANCY CREEK

FANCY CREEK
STATE PARK

RANDOLPH BRIDGE

RANDOLPH
STATE PARK

BALDWIN CREEK
RECREATION
AREA

DRY CREEK

GARRISON
RECREATION
AREA

HOHMAN CEMETERY

LANDING
STRIP

CARNAHAN CEMETERY

CARNAHAN GARRISON
RECREATION AREA

STOCKDALE
RECREATION AREA

BIG BLUE RIVER

MILL CREEK

JEEP TRAIL

177
24

TUTTLE
CREEK
LAKE

SPILLWAY

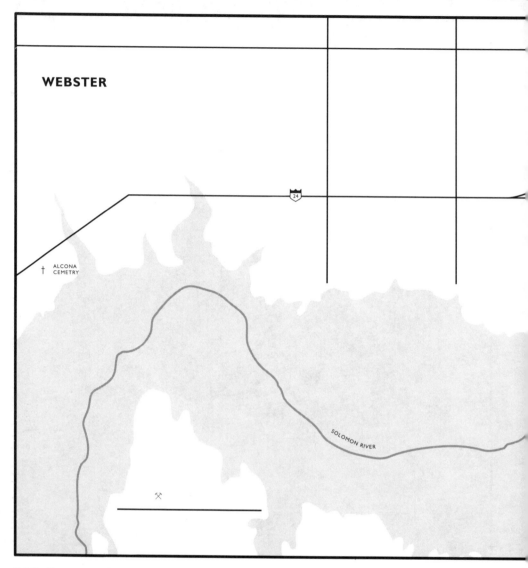

WEBSTER

✝ ALCONA
CEMETERY

SOLOMON RIVER

Webster Reservoir

Like other reservoirs in the far west, Webster is not likely to ever again reach its conservation pool level of 1,890 feet above sea level. Heavy irrigation has lowered the region's water table, and Webster has averaged a pool level of about 1,870 in recent years. In addition, heavy siltation has raised the bottom, further reducing the reservoir's depth.

Even so, Webster's walleye population was thriving after enjoying relatively high water levels in the late 1980s. Reproductive success appeared good on the gravel bottoms at each end of the dam, and along

the bluffs, and the average size of mature walleye was four to six pounds, according to district fisheries biologist Steve Price.

Price was working to establish a minimum water level at the lake for wildlife and recreation, so that irrigators could no longer draw it down below the irrigation pool. When Webster is drawn way down, it loses entire year classes of fish, he said.

Some 360,000 wiper fry were stocked at Webster in 1990 and Price had high hopes for the hybrids. "I think the wipers are going to do real well, with the exception of a severe irrigation drawdown," he said.

Webster is home to a tremendous gizzard shad population, providing the wip-

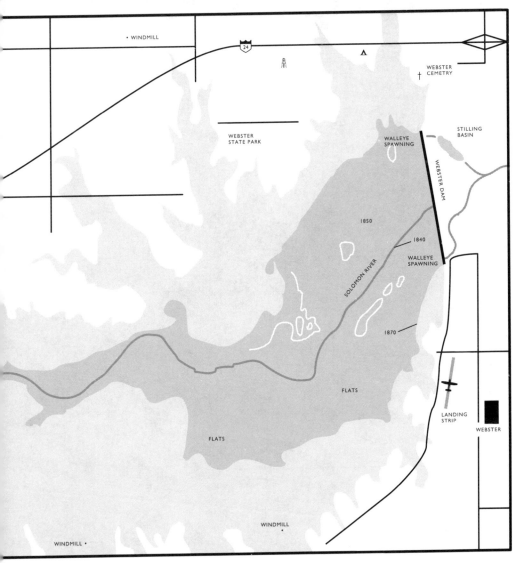

ers with plenty of forage. Price was hoping the wipers would get established in the lake before white bass did — someone slipped whites into the lake in the late '80s, much to the biologist's dismay.

Crappie populations have been fair in recent years and were on the way up in 1990. Flathead fishing was good in the reservoirs, with many flathead caught incidentally by walleye fishermen drifting the mudflats on the south side of the lake in May and June. Setline fishing is good at the same time of year in deep water along the bluffs.

Largemouth bass fishing varies widely from year to year — generally rising and falling with the water level in the reservoir. A 15-inch length limit applies.

The five-acre stilling basin below Webster Dam offers an interesting variety of angling opportunities. Rainbow trout are stocked late in the fall for cool-weather fishing. The basin also holds smallmouth bass, redear sunfish and channel cats. An 18-inch length limit on smallmouth preserves the fish. "Essentially, it's catch and release," Price said.

For up to date fishing information, call the Wildlife and Parks office at Webster State Park, (913) 425-6775.

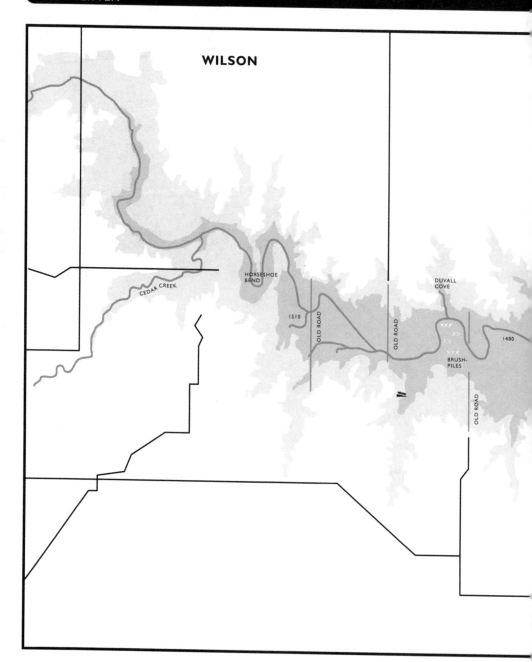

WILSON

HORSESHOE BEND

CEDAR CREEK

DUVALL COVE

1510

OLD ROAD

OLD ROAD

1480

BRUSH-PILES

OLD ROAD

Wilson Lake

The coolest, clearest and deepest lake in Kansas, Wilson also offers better fishing for more species than any other reservoir except, perhaps, Glen Elder.

By far the best lake in the state for striper fishing, Wilson also ranks at or near the top for walleye, smallmouth bass and white bass. If that weren't enough, excellent spring largemouth fishing can be found in Wilson's streams, although Kansans accustomed to murkier waters often find the reservoir difficult to adjust to.

The area off Lucas Point is rich in structural diversity and a favorite hangout of striped bass, as is the river channel area off Rocktown Cove. Stripers cruise the channel, heading up rocky points to feed in shallower waters at night. They also lurk in the dropoffs below rocky humps, including an underwater cliff near the dam outlet structure.

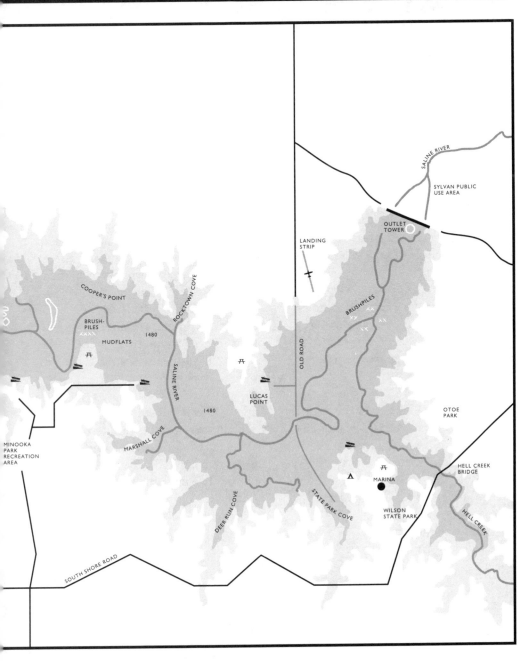

Found throughout the lake in winter months, stripers stick to the deep eastern half in summer. Troll shiny or sparkling deep-swimming spoons, crankbaits, jigs and minnows of blue, silver, pink and white. Downriggers are excellent tools for lowering lures to striper depths. Slab spoons and live bait, such as bluegill, large minnows or small white bass, work well when fishing directly over fish suspended at the edge of a river channel or hump.

Live bait probably works best when casting from shore for stripers during evening, nighttime and early morning hours.

Humps and rocky points are favorite spots for walleye, white bass and smallmouth bass as well. Sometimes, by dangling slab spoons and jigs tipped with bait just off the bottom, you can catch all four species in the same place at the same time.

Walleye spawn in wind-swept shallows

off gravel points throughout the lake's eastern half, and not just along the dam, as is the case at many reservoirs. Walleye also congregate off Pelican Point — just west of the housing development on the lake's eastern shore. They like old road beds, switchbacks in the river channel and a hole above the bridge in Hell Creek Cove.

Mudflats run from a pile of brush off Minooka Point to the river channel at the mouth of Rocktown Cove. A river switchback at Duvall Cove also features brush, dropoffs, an old roadbed and other fine walleye structure.

Smallmouth can be found along the dam, off rocky points and in Rocktown Cove. Anglers often catch smallmouth while fishing for walleye and whites. Smallmouth will hit minnows, worms, crankbaits ands crayfish.

White bass roam all over the lake and can sometimes be spotted by watching for surfacing schools of frantic shad or diving gulls and terns. Even if the fish are no longer near top when you arrive at the spot, dangle slab spoons off the bottom there and you're likely to find immediate action.

White bass make spring spawning runs up the river and provide superior ice fish-ing action when conditions permit.

Completed in 1964, the Wilson dam is nearly a mile long and rises 160 feet above the stream bed. It lies in post-rock country, where settlers carved fence posts out of limestone rather than wood, which is scarce in the area. Old post-rock fence rows, if you can find them, sometimes attract fish.

At conservation pool, Wilson boasts 9,000 surface acres and 100 miles of shoreline. But water levels can vary markedly from year to year. For daily lake level and release flow information, contact the Kansas City U.S. Army Corps of Engineers office at (816) 374-5241.

In addition to a State Park of nearly 800 acres, Wilson sports excellent Corps of Engineers boat ramps, complete with fish-cleaning stations. Channel cats often linger around the cleaning stations. Wilson's marina offers boat rentals. The State Park number is (913) 658-2465.

Rocktown Cove was the first area in the state preserved permanently as a natural area rich in biological and historical heritage. The Bur Oak Nature Trail, below the dam and adjacent to Sylvan Park, is accessible to folks with physical handicaps.

ALL SURFACE WATERS in Kansas drain toward the Mississippi, but they travel on two distinct paths. To picture how the waters flow in Kansas, divide the state roughly into northern and southern halves. ✏ Streams in the north, anchored by the Kansas River and its tributaries, empty into the Missouri, while streams in the south generally feed the Arkansas. The systems don't meet until their waters mix in the Mississippi. The main exception to this rule lies in the southeast, where three tributaries to the Osage River — the Marais des Cygnes, Little Osage and Marmaton — spurn the Ark for the Missouri.

Fish populations don't follow the same divisions as the rivers. To picture how the fish travel, divide the state again — this time into eastern and western halves.

Streams in the dry west are often intermittent, running high in spring or after heavy rains but going dry during droughts. This cycle has been greatly exacerbated since the 1960s by farm irrigation systems, which have pumped out the groundwater that recharges streams, creating man-made drought conditions. Outside of impoundments, there are only a few streams in the west that offer anything other than occasional fishing opportunities.

By contrast, excellent fishing can be found year-round in many central and eastern streams. This is especially true in the clear rivers and brooks of the Flint Hills and southeast Kansas.

No matter what the sign says, you don't see the "Scenic Flint Hills" from the Kansas Turnpike. You have to leave the Interstate for roads more in tune with the landscape, like Kansas 177, which winds up, down and among the hills, passing lush green bean fields and streams lined with cottonwood trees, whose leaves dance with the breeze as they wink at the sun.

Lazy cattle lie in pastures while chocolate-colored horses graze and flick their tails at flies. Meadowlarks stretch their necks to sing from fenceposts as prairie chickens burst from roadside grasses.

Spring waters run knee-high over a low-water bridge in a valley between the hills. Wearing shorts and tennis shoes, an angler wades into the stream and casts lures to the edge of bank undercuts, fallen trees and rock bars — domain of the spotted bass. Tall trees tower toward a bright blue sky; a woodpecker hammers into one of them.

Wildlife biologist Rick Tush loves these central Flint Hills streams, where he releases turkeys, counts quail and comes to fish in the evening hours. He owns no land along the rivers and creeks, which rarely meander across public property. But when Tush sees a stretch of stream he likes, he seeks out the landowner.

"I'm straight with them," he says. "I tell

them I like to fish and I understand they own that part of the creek and I was wondering if I could try the fishing on it."

Tush pauses for a moment, staring ahead. "I'm sorry," he finally says. "I'm just trying to remember if anyone's ever turned me down."

If so, he couldn't remember it.

Tush casts a plastic worm into a hole beneath an old stone bridge and starts battling a two-pound spotted bass. Often called Kentucky bass, the spotted features a splotchy dark line across its flank, with the splotches sometimes diamond shaped. Under this line run rows of small spots. Its mouth ends under the center of the eye, unlike the largemouth, which extends behind the eye, or the smallmouth, which barely reaches the eye.

Spotted bass are native to both the Flint Hills streams that flow toward the Arkansas River and the Osage tributaries in the Missouri River drainage. They are not native, however, to streams draining into the Kansas, or "Kaw," River. That is one of the major differences in the Kansas and Arkansas river systems, from an angler's view, and it is one of several advantages that southeast streams have over those elsewhere in the state.

The streams of the southeast also tend to be cleaner. Cool, clear spring waters flow through limestone and gravel filters before discharging into the stream basins. Rainwater rolls mainly off of grassland, where it picks up very little dirt on its downhill run to the rivers, unlike in the northeast, where tons of topsoil are washed each year off of cultivated croplands.

In addition, the southeast gets more rainfall than any other region in Kansas.

The most varied stream fishing in the state can be found deep in the southeast corner, around Galena's Empire Lake. There, in Kansas' own little piece of the Ozarks, all three black bass species roam in Shoal Creek and the Spring River.

Spotted bass especially like the upper headwaters of these cool, clear rock-bottomed streams, while largemouth prefer the lower, wider sections.

The Spring River system supports what is likely the only native smallmouth bass population in Kansas — all other waters boasting smallmouth were stocked. Stream smallmouth prefer pools with undercut banks and cover, such as fallen trees or large boulders. They hunt for crayfish, aquatic insects and baitfish in nearby riffles and gravel-bottomed shallows.

Shoal Creek also may be the only spot in Kansas to harbor a native population of rock bass — a scrappy, red-eyed sunfish that resembles the black crappie in color and size but fights harder and doesn't taste as good.

North of Spring River, the clean, narrow Little Osage and Marmaton Rivers also offer Ozark-style fishing for spotted and largemouth bass. However, there are no public access sites to the Little Osage and only one to the Marmaton — at a low-water dam in Fort Scott. Landowner permission must be obtained before testing either of the streams, which also offer excellent fishing for flathead and channel catfish.

Public access is better to the fertile Marais des Cygnes River, which flows approximately seven miles through a State Wildlife Area. Largemouth bass, which are native to the Marais des Cygnes and its tributaries, tend to outcompete spotted bass there, especially in relatively dry years when waters are less turbid. Sauger also are native to the Marais des Cygnes and can be caught with the same techniques used on walleye. One of the only rivers in Kansas still visited by blue catfish, the Marais des Cygnes harbors other giants as well, including the strange and ancient paddlefish and the bigmouth buffalo. Flathead and channel cat fishing are excellent in the river and its tributary creeks.

Moving west, the Neosho River is famous for its huge flatheads, especially in its southern reaches. An 86 pound, 3 ounce flathead caught near St. Paul by Ray Wiechert stood as the state record for 24 years before it was finally topped in 1990 by an 87.5 pound fish taken out of Pomona Reservoir, a pool in the Marais des Cygnes system.

Walleye can be found in the upper Neosho watershed, which includes Council Grove Reservoir and City Lake. Largemouth and spotted bass are common in the Neosho and its tributaries, which include the gorgeous Cottonwood River — a centerpiece attraction of the Flint Hills. The Cottonwood's South Fork and Cedar Creek tributaries offer some of the state's finest fishing for spotted bass.

Spotted bass range throughout the Verdigris River and its tributaries, yielding to largemouth in the lower mainstream sections. Large channel and flathead catfish abound in the Verdigris system, which includes Fall and Elk Rivers, Big Creek and four major reservoirs: Toronto, Fall River, Elk City and Big Hill.

Public access to streams is generally available above and below reservoirs. One of the most scenic stretches in the state lies on the upper Fall River, between Eureka and the reservoir, where the stream winds through several miles of wooded valley owned or leased by the state. A fine spot to launch a canoe, this stretch of Fall River harbors spotted and largemouth bass, as well as flathead and channel catfish. In early spring, white bass head up the river and its Otter Creek tributary to spawn, though their run is not as spectacular as it once was.

The West Branch of Fall River is a classic Flint Hills Stream, boasting spotted and largemouth bass. Spotted bass appear to be falling behind the largemouth along the West Branch in recent years, possibly because numerous dams in the drainage have evened out the stream's flow, decreasing turbidity and causing fewer deep holes

to be scoured out by raging spring floodwaters. Spotted bass thrive in fast streams with deep holes, while largemouth do just fine in shallow, sedentary waters. In addition, largemouth have been stocked in most every pond and watershed lake in the river's drainage area, so they may be overwhelming spotted bass with sheer numbers alone.

The Caney River flows out of the Chautauqua Hills toward Oklahoma's Hulah Reservoir. Mile for mile, the Caney may be the most beautiful stretch of water in Kansas. It features natural waterfalls, numerous riffles and a few rapids of medium difficulty for springtime canoe paddlers. Public access points are available at Grenola and in the Hulah Wildlife Area outside Elgin. Spotted and largemouth bass call the river home, as do white bass, channel cats and flatheads.

The same species can be found among settings of nearly equal beauty in nearby Beaver Creek, Grouse Creek and the lower Walnut River. All three streams gurgle gently beneath tall hardwood canopies that harbor chirping songbirds and buzzing insects. Glaring patches of reflected sunlight gleam off the riffles. Imagine that the oaks and cottonwoods are maples, pines and aspen and you'd swear you were fishing on a northern trout stream, particularly if you are using a fly rod. Flies can be deadly at dawn and dusk on surface-feeding bass. They also work well on green sunfish, hiding among brush, and will trick an occasional channel cat.

Fishing for largemouth bass, walleye, green sunfish, white crappie, flatheads and channel cats is good in northeast Kansas on the Kaw, west of Lawrence, and on many of its tributaries. Worthy of special note are Mill Creek, Lyons Creek and Deep Creek. Deep Creek not only harbors largemouth bass, but also some stocked spotted bass.

Blue cats still venture up the Kansas River from their home base in the Missouri now and again, including an 82-pound blue caught at De Soto in 1988 by Preston Stubbs, Jr. Although Stubbs' fish ranks as a state record, blue cats of 200 and even 300 pounds swam in Kansas a century and a half ago, according to the reports of early white settlers. A 315-pound blue catfish was taken from the Missouri River in 1866.

Rare catches of native sauger are made in the Kansas River and its tributaries, as far west as the Big Blue. Far more common are walleye that have escaped from reservoirs.

Curiously enough, the largest wipers in the state have been turning up in recent years below Milford Reservoir, even though wiper stockings have not been a part of Milford's past. Because wipers are a sterile hybrid, biologists believe the fish escaped other reservoirs, such as Kanopolis, and then traveled through the Kansas River system up the Republican River to the Milford spillway. A record 18 pound, 15 ounce wiper was caught there by Lone Bounsombath in 1990. When water levels permit, the southern stretch of the Republican also supports one of the state's highest concentrations of big flatheads.

White bass, crappie, walleye and largemouth bass swim upstream of reservoirs in eastern and central Kansas during their respective spawning seasons.

Excellent spring fishing for white bass and good year-round fishing for channel catfish can be found in the streams feeding into Glen Elder, Wilson and Kanopolis Reservoirs.

The Smoky Hill, east and west of Kanopolis, offers some of the state's best stream fishing for flatheads. During the drought of 1988, for instance, when flatheads were concentrated in deep pools, a group of four fishermen took 11 catfish weighing a total of 478 pounds from three holes in the Smoky Hill. That's an average weight of 43½ pounds per fish; the largest weighed 62 pounds.

Pools in the Arkansas River formed by dams in Wichita harbor large flatheads and channel cats. In the city limits, the Ark is sometimes stocked with largemouth, channel cats and a winter supply of rainbow trout for put-and-take fishing. The Ark becomes an intermittent stream a few miles west of Wichita and dries out completely west of Great Bend for years at a time, with the exception of occasional dribbles from spring runoffs and heavy rains.

White bass once made exceptional spawning runs from Cheney Reservoir up the North Fork of the Ninnescah every April. However, a buildup of silt where the river meets the lake, plus an abundance of alternative spawning sites around the reservoir, prompted the white bass to change their habits. As a result, not much has been running between the banks of the North Fork in recent Aprils except water. But the water itself was something Ken Brunson, state stream fisheries biologist, didn't take for granted.

"We protected this stream with 1985 legislation," Brunson said one morning as he stood knee deep in the North Fork, casting yellow jigs for white bass without success. "It got early action, because this is the cutting edge. If we can stop the problem here, then we've proved that we can do something. It's too late for some of the other western Kansas rivers."

Central-pivot irrigation systems, which

Minimum stream flow laws have been passed to protect some western rivers from being pumped dry by irrigation.

utilize groundwater pumped up from wells, have reduced the flow of many western streams to a seasonal trickle since becoming popular with farmers in the 1970s. The problem arises when so many people are allowed to take water from a stream, or the aquifer recharging it, that the stream dries up.

State Water Plan legislation establishing minimum stream flows began to offers minimal protection to 18 streams, including the North Fork, in the 1980s. Perhaps more important, Brunson says, the minimum stream flow regulations attracted public attention to "the artificial de-watering of streams."

Unfortunately, some valuable streams — most notably the western Kansas

stretch of the Arkansas River — had to be lost before attitudes about regulating stream flows and groundwater use began to change.

Good fishing for largemouth bass and channel catfish can still be found in Pratt County tributaries to the Ninnescah, in the Chikaskia River system of Kingman and Sumner Counties, and in the Medicine Lodge River system in Barber, Pratt and Kiowa Counties. West of this, occasional fishing opportunities are offered in springtime by streams carrying heavy runoff. Otherwise, fishing is limited to the short stretches of stream lying on either side of western Kansas impoundments.

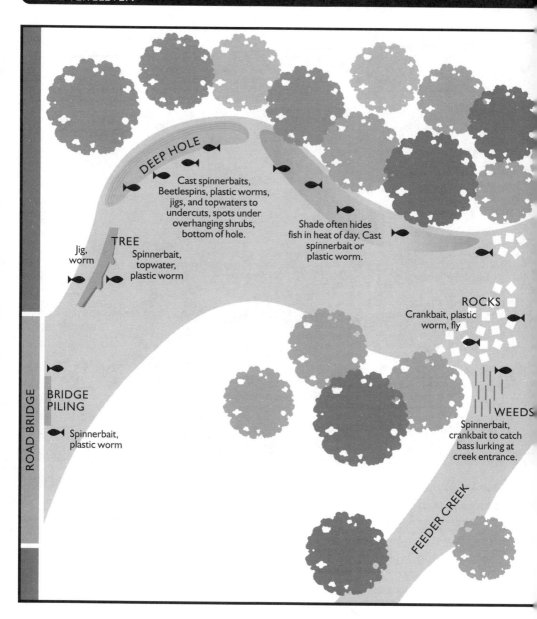

DEEP HOLE
Cast spinnerbaits, Beetlespins, plastic worms, jigs, and topwaters to undercuts, spots under overhanging shrubs, bottom of hole.

Shade often hides fish in heat of day. Cast spinnerbait or plastic worm.

Jig, worm

TREE
Spinnerbait, topwater, plastic worm

ROCKS
Crankbait, plastic worm, fly

ROAD BRIDGE

BRIDGE PILING
Spinnerbait, plastic worm

WEEDS
Spinnerbait, crankbait to catch bass lurking at creek entrance.

FEEDER CREEK

A Flint Hills Bass Stream

Wade or fish in a float tube to catch spotted bass, largemouth and green sunfish.

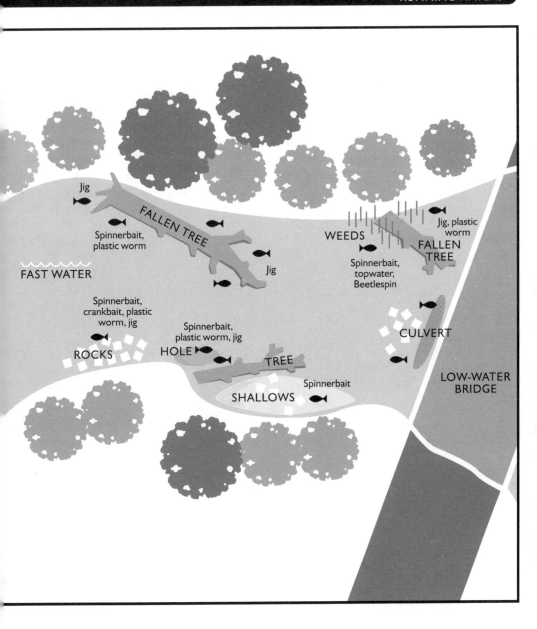

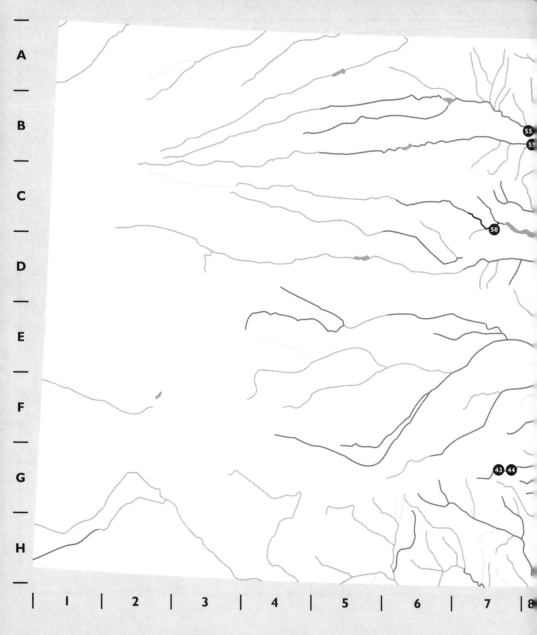

Kansas Rivers and Streams

Use this map in conjunction with any travel map of Kansas to find access points to the state's rivers and streams.

〜 Highest-valued fishery resource

〜 High-priority fishery resource

〜 Moderate fishery resource

〜 Limited fishery resource

STREAM PUBLIC ACCESS POINTS

1. **Arkansas River,** 21st St. Bridge, Wichita (F-10)

2. **Arkansas River,** Lincoln St. Bridge, Wichita (G-10)

3. **Arkansas River,** low water dam at Oxford (G-10)

4. **Arkansas River,** at Geuda Springs (H-10)

5. **Arkansas River,** at Arkansas City (H-10)

6. **Arkansas River,** above Kaw Reservoir, Cowley Co. (G-10)

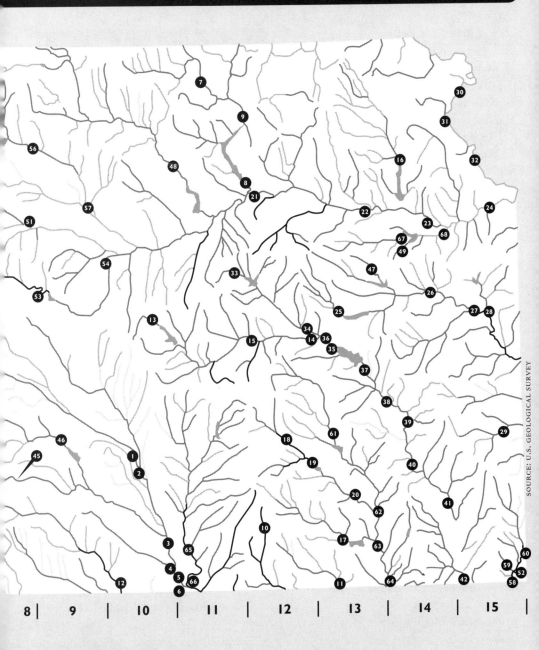

SOURCE: U.S. GEOLOGICAL SURVEY

8 | 9 | 10 | 11 | 12 | 13 | 14 | 15 |

7. **Blue (Little) River,** 1 mile west, 6 miles south of Hanover (A-12)

8. **Big Blue River,** Rocky Ford Dam, Manhattan (C-11)

9. **Big Blue River,** above Tuttle Creek Reservoir (B-11)

10. **Caney River,** at Grenola (G-12)

11. **Caney (Little) River,** low water dam at Caney (H-13)

12. **Chikaskia River,** Drury Dam, 5½ miles west of South Haven (H-10)

13. **Cottonwood River,** above Marion Reservoir (D-10)

14. **Cottonwood River,** low water dam at Emporia (E-12)

15. **Cottonwood River,** at Cottonwood Falls (F-11)

16. **Delaware River,** above Perry Reservoir at Valley Falls (B-13)

17. **Elk River,** above Elk City Reservoir (H-13)

18. **Fall River,** at Eureka (F-12)

19. **Fall River,** above Fall River Reservoir (F-12)

20. **Fall River,** low water dam at Fredonia (G-13)

21. **Kansas (Kaw) River,** at mouth of Big Blue, Manhattan (C-12)

22. **Kansas River,** at Topeka (C-13)

23. **Kansas River,** at Lawrence (C-14)

24. **Kansas River,** at Edwardsville (C-15)

25. **Marais des Cygnes River,** above Melvern Reservoir (D-13)

26. **Marais des Cygnes River,** low water dam at Ottawa (D-14)

27. **Marais des Cygnes River,** low water dam at Osawatomie (E-15)

28. **Marais des Cygnes River,** on Marais des Cygnes Wildlife Area, (E-15)

29. **Marmaton River,** low water dam at Fort Scott (F-15)

30. **Missouri River,** most city parks in Doniphan, Atchison, Leavenworth and Wyandotte Counties (B-14)

31. **Missouri River,** at Atchison (B-15)

32. **Missouri River,** at Leavenworth (C-14)

33. **Neosho River,** above Council Grove Reservoir (D-11)

34. **Neosho River,** low water dam at Emporia (E-12)

35. **Neosho River,** low water dam at Hartford (E-13)

36. **Neosho River,** above John Redmond Reservoir (E-13)

37. **Neosho River,** low water dam at Burlington (E-13)

38. **Neosho River,** low water dam at Neosho Falls (F-13)

39. **Neosho River,** low water dam at Iola (F-14)

40. **Neosho River,** low water dam at Chanute (G-14)

41. **Neosho River,** at Neosho Wildlife Area (G-14)

42. **Neosho River,** low water dam at Chetopa (H-15)

43. **Ninnescah River (South Fork),** Lemon Park in Pratt (G-7)

44. **Ninnescah River (South Fork),** Two miles east, one mile south of Pratt (G-7)

45. **Ninnescah River (South Fork),** at Byron Walker Wildlife Area and

Good fishing for largemouth bass can be had in many Kansas tributaries.

Kingman State Fishing Lake (F-8)

46. **Ninnescah River (North Fork),** above Cheney Reservoir (F-9)

47. **One Hundred and Ten Mile Creek,** above Pomona Reservoir (D-13)

48. **Republican River,** above and below Milford Reservoir (C-11)

49. **Rock Creek,** above Clinton Reservoir (C-14)

50. **Saline River,** above Wilson Reservoir (C-7)

51. **Saline River,** low-water dam at Lincoln (C-8)

52. **Shoal Creek,** at Galena (H-15)

53. **Smoky Hill River,** above Kanopolis Reservoir (D-9)

54. **Smoky Hill River,** at Salina (D-10)

55. **Solomon River (North and South Forks),** above Glen Elder Reservoir (B-8)

56. **Solomon River,** at Beloit (B-9)

57. **Solomon River,** low water dam in Minneapolis (C-9)

58. **Spring River,** low water dam at Baxter Springs (H-15)

59. **Spring River,** southeast of Riverton below Empire Lake (H-15)

60. **Spring River,** off K-96 near the Kansas/Missouri State Line (H-15)

61. **Verdigris River,** above Toronto Reservoir (F-13)

62. **Verdigris River,** low water dam at Neodesha (G-13)

63. **Verdigris River,** low water dams at Independence (H-13)

64. **Verdigris River,** low water dams at Coffeyville (H-14)

65. **Walnut River,** at Winfield (H-11)

66. **Walnut River,** at Arkansas City (H-10)

67. **Wakarusa River,** above Clinton Reservoir (C-14)

68. **Wakarusa River,** at Eudora (C-14)

D EVELOPED WITH THE HELP of fishing license revenues and excise taxes on angling equipment, Kansas State Fishing Lakes are managed by the Department of Wildlife and Parks primarily for fishing, and not necessarily for multiple-use recreation. 🐟 Waterskiing, recreational motorboating and swimming are usually prohibited. Activities that tend not to interfere with fishing — including sailing, paddle-boating and canoeing — are permitted. Most lakes have boat ramps, fishing piers and outhouses; rough camping is free. Few state lakes have garbage cans, so bring enough bags to haul out what you bring in. 🐟 Small in comparison with major reservoirs, state fishing lakes are more likely to lose their gamefish populations to overfishing or to dramatic weather events, such as a summer-long drought. Fish numbers and the balances between species can change tremendously from year to year. Drawdowns are required from time to time to eliminate rough fish and restore stands of food and cover vegetation for gamefish species. 🐟 Only general descriptions of the state fishing lakes are included in this chapter. For updates on specific lakes, contact Wildlife and Parks regional offices.

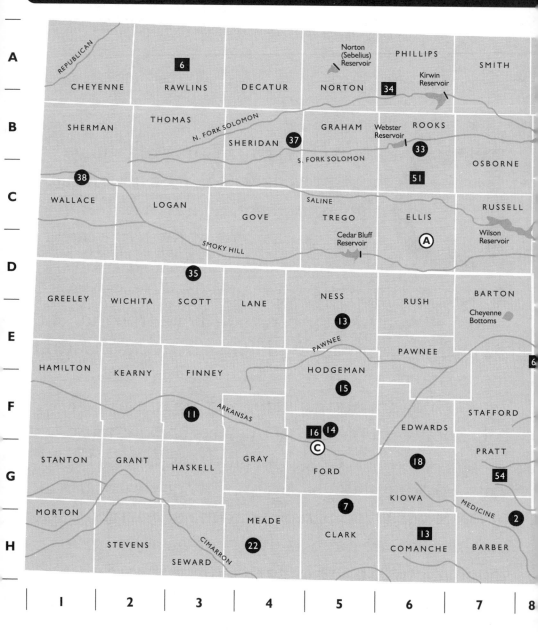

Little Lakes

- 🄳 State fishing lake
- 🄳 Community lake

Wildlife & Parks Regional Offices:

- Ⓐ Reg. 1 (NW), Hays (913) 628-8614
- Ⓑ Reg. 2 (NE), Topeka (913) 273-6740
- Ⓒ Reg. 3 (SW), Dodge City (316) 227-8609
- Ⓓ Reg. 4 (SC), Valley Center (316) 755-2711
- Ⓔ Reg. 5 (SE), Chanute (316) 431-0380

STATE FISHING LAKES

1. **Atchison** (B-14). A 69-acre lake surrounded by 179 acres of public land, Atchison harbors crappie, largemouth bass, channel catfish, bluegill, walleye, sunfish and flathead catfish, as well as the less welcome common carp and bullhead. Rough camping, drinking water and picnic areas are available at the lake, four miles north and two miles west of Atchison.

2. **Barber** (G-8). Just north of Medicine Lodge, quiet Barber lake is an excellent

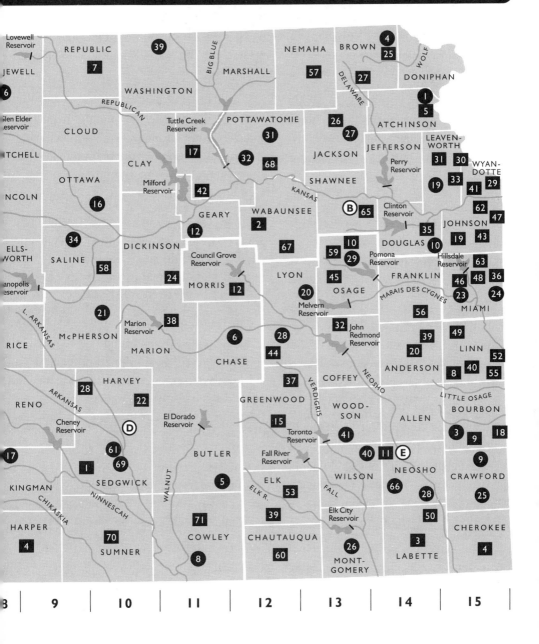

spot to flyfish in the shallows for bluegill and sunfish. Crappie, largemouth bass and channel cats also reside in the 77-acre lake, ringed by 113 acres of public land. Barber offers rough camping, picnic areas and drinking water.

3. **Bourbon** (F-15). Spreading out over 100 acres during times of normal rainfall, Bourbon has largemouth bass, crappie, bluegill, channel cats, walleye, sunfish, bullhead and possibly a few northern pike. Rough camping, drinking water and picnic

areas are available, four miles east of Elsmore and 19 miles west of Fort Scott.

4. **Brown** (A-14). Concessions and boat rentals — in addition to camping, drinking water and picnic areas — are available at 60-acre Brown Lake in the northeast corner of Kansas. Largemouth bass, channel catfish, crappie, bluegill, flatheads and sunfish swim in Brown, eight miles east and one mile south of Hiawatha. Brown is surrounded by 127 acres of public land.

5. **Butler** (G-11). "When people are look-

ing for a place to get away from the crowds, I send them to Butler State Fishing Lake," said district fisheries biologist Ron Marteney.

Butler has been known to offer excellent early-spring fishing for largemouth bass, which often lurk within casting distance of the lake's fishing piers. A few large northern pike — longer than the statewide minimum of 30 inches — also roam in the lake, three miles west and one mile north of Latham. Channel cats and panfish are usually plentiful.

At least as impressive as the fishing at the 124-acre lake are the 227 acres of gently rolling prairie around it. In early summer, when the southern Flint Hills come into full bloom, wildflowers of blue, white, purple, pink, red, orange and yellow wave among the green grasses. Fenced off from grazing cattle, Butler remains a pristine piece of tallgrass prairie.

Thanks to their rich habitat, the lands around Butler Lake house coveys of whistling quail, screeching killdeer, flocks of doves and chattering upland sandpipers that divebomb to landings on fencepost perches and then slowly tuck in their wings. The lake's marshy shallows also attract scores of swimming snakes, which aren't poisonous but have frightened the waders off more than one float-tube fishermen.

6. **Chase** (E-12). Rumored to be one of the few small lakes in Kansas supporting smallmouth, Chase has not produced many of the scrappy bronze bass in recent years. But spotted bass, which are native to the Flint Hills and fight just as hard as smallmouth, are still taken from time to time. Swimming is allowed at his 109-acre lake, and you'll know why if you fish there in the heat of summer. Better to ply the waters of Chase in spring and fall, or on cool summer nights, when largemouth bass, channel cats, crappie and walleye rise to feed. Located 1½ miles west of Cottonwood Falls, smack in the middle of the

lovely Flint Hills, Chase is ringed by 383 acres of public property. Camping, drinking water and picnic areas are available.

7. **Clark** (G-5). One of the state's biggest surprises, Clark Lake appears out of nowhere on the dry and dusty high plains — a glittering mirage, 300 acres across and 42 feet deep. Clark rests at the bottom of a stunning canyon. Atop the bluffs lies a wild west county populated, for the most part, by antelope, mule deer, lesser prairie chickens, wild turkeys and coyotes. Migrating eagles and ospreys often stop by Clark Lake to fish.

Largemouth bass hide in the flooded timber at the north end of the lake and in the feeder creeks. Stream channels, as they enter the main lake, also are good spots to look for largemouth.

White bass roam the deep south half of the 337-acre reservoir, chasing schools of gizzard shad. Occasional walleye are caught near springs entering the lake from the west. Channel catfish are abundant and crappie are common in the rock-walled lake.

Clark offers a limited number of rough camping sites. A concession stand-bait shop burned down in 1989 and there was some question as to whether or not it would be rebuilt.

Surrounded by 900 acres of public land, Clark lies 10 miles south of Kingsdown. You won't see it until you get there.

8. **Cowley** (H-11). Recently drawn down to stimulate the growth of food and cover plants, Cowley Lake boasts some of the clearest waters in Kansas. Most of the rainwater that winds up in the lake flows off of pastureland meadows whose soils are held firmly in place by prairie grasses and wildflowers. Very little loose dirt hitches a ride with the runoff as it rolls into Panther Creek and then the lake.

Cowley may be too clean, in fact, to ever become a top bass lake. It doesn't hold the high level of nutrients common in a highly productive food chain.

But Cowley is a beautiful lake of 84 acres, encircled by tall trees, limestone bluffs and prairie meadows. Largemouth can be caught there, particularly after recent rains stir up the water a bit. Look for them around the bluffs across from the boat ramp, off the point between the lake's two arms and in the first cove north of the dam. Bluegills, sunfish and crappie numbers are usually good and spotted bass are caught on occasion. Ringed by 113 acres of public land, Cowley lies 15 miles east of Arkansas City.

9. **Crawford** (G-15). Largemouth bass, crappie, channel cats, bluegill, sunfish and spotted bass roam in this 150-acre lake three miles northeast of Farlington.

10. **Douglas** (D-14). Boat rentals and concessions are available at Douglas Lake, 1½ miles north and 1 mile east of Baldwin. Largemouth bass, channel catfish, bluegill, sunfish and a few walleye swim along with the carp and bullhead in this 180-acre lake surrounded by 538 acres of public land.

11. **Finney (Concannon)** (F-3). About one-fifth its original size at 60 acres, this lake has suffered from the declining groundwater levels brought on by increased irrigation in the southwest. Call the regional Wildlife and Parks office in Dodge City to check on conditions before planning an outing to a lake that might not be there.

12. **Geary** (C-11). Channel catfish, largemouth bass, bluegill, walleye and crappie frequent this 96-acre lake bordered by 355 acres. Rough camping, drinking water and picnic areas are available at Geary, 8½ miles south and one mile west of Junction City.

13. **Goodman** (E-5). This new 40-acre lake about five miles southeast of Ness City had already lost half of its water by 1990, two years after it opened. Goodman was stocked with largemouth, channel cats, redear sunfish and bluegill, but state biologists suspect it will be a constant struggle to maintain the fishery in a place where waters rarely flow.

14. **Hain** (F-5). A spartan little lake, five miles west of Spearville, Hain harbors catfish and bullhead, crappie and largemouth. Rough camping is available, but bring your own drinking water.

15. **Hodgeman** (F-5). An 87-acre basin five miles southeast of Jetmore, Hodgeman has an uncertain supply of water and fish. Call the Dodge City district office for an update, or wait for a wet year.

16. **Jewell** (A-8). Largemouth bass, bluegill, channel cats and green sunfish can be found at this 57-acre lake in north-central Kansas, six miles south and three miles west of Mankato. Camping, water and picnic tables are offered on 108 acres of public land.

17. **Kingman** (G-8). Folks pitching tents or spreading picnic blankets on the scenic shores of Kingman Lake can thank Byron Walker for their shade.

"Those big trees on the east side of the lake — I planted them the first year I moved here," says Walker, who managed the lake and adjacent wildlife area for 40 years, starting in 1947.

In 1984, Kingman was drained, flooded and restocked for the fourth time in 54 years. Excellent fishing for largemouth bass and walleye could be found there in 1987 and 1988.

Unfortunately, at 185 acres, Kingman is highly vulnerable to excess fishing pressure and sustained severe weather, such as the '88 drought. When fishing is good, anglers who want to return to Kingman should practice catch-and-release on bass and walleye.

A lovely spot to while away a morning, Kingman lures migrating eagles, ducks, geese and, on occasion, sandhill cranes. Though heavily hunted in the fall, the surrounding 4,500-acre Byron Walker Wildlife Area harbors bobwhite quail, wild turkeys, deer, doves and other wildlife through the spring and summer. Rough camping is available along the lakeshore. Several ponds holding small bass and panfish dot the wildlife area, although you should expect to negotiate patches of poison ivy, chiggers and ticks to reach them.

18. **Kiowa** (G-6). A 22-acre lake at the northwest edge of Greensburg, Kiowa holds largemouth bass, channel cats and sunfish. Drinking water, picnic tables and grills are available on 21 acres of adjacent parkland.

19. **Leavenworth** (C-14). Nestled among beautiful rolling hills and hardwood forests, Leavenworth lies three miles west and one mile north of Tonganoxie. Channel cats, largemouth bass, crappie, bluegill and sunfish live in the 175-acre lake, which is surrounded by 332 acres of public land. Concessions and boat rentals are available.

20. **Lyon** (D-13). Channel cats, largemouth bass, sunfish, plus a few walleye swim in this 135-acre lake, five miles west and one mile north of Reading. Swimming is allowed at Lyon, ringed by 447 acres of public land. The usual rough campsites, well water and picnic tables can be found.

21. **McPherson** (E-10). Surrounded by the state's largest game refuge, McPherson Lake and the associated Maxwell Wildlife Area offer a rare glimpse of what Kansas used to be. Just an hour or so north of Wichita, the state's largest city, you can camp for free under tall trees beside a pretty lake surrounded by hills where elk and buffalo again roam across the prairie.

McPherson holds so many largemouth bass that their growth is stunted and a 12-to-15-inch slot length limit applies. Biologist Gordon Schneider hopes anglers will remove fish under 12 inches for the benefit of the survivors. Fish over 15 inches may also be taken home, and a few do lurk in the vicinity.

Channel catfish and bluegill also can be caught at McPherson, six miles north and two miles west of Canton. But once you're under the spell of the area — where thick-necked elk hold noses high and antlers back; where bison bulls face off in the middle of the road; where red-tailed hawks screech, kingbirds swoop and bluebirds chirp from fencepost perches — the fishing often becomes secondary.

22. **Meade** (H-4). A 100-acre oasis in southwest Kansas, Lake Meade is encircled by tall, thick-trunked oaks and cottonwoods. A State Park, and not technically a fishing lake, Meade offers a swimming beach, electrical hookups and lovely campsites. Largemouth bass can be found in weedy shallows and off the points; channel catfish and redear sunfish abound. The lake lies eight miles south and five miles west of the town of Meade.

23. **Miami** (D-15). A nice-sized area featuring 267 acres of water, Miami harbors largemouth bass, channel cats, crappie and sunfish. Rough camping and picnic sites can be found, but bring your own drinking water. Miami Lake is eight miles east and five miles south of Osawatomie.

24. **Middle Creek (Louisburg)** (D-15). A 280-acre lake and wildlife area featuring channel and flathead catfish, largemouth and spotted bass, white bass, crappie and bluegill.

25. **Mined Land Area Strip Pits** (G-15). Long and narrow, clear and deep, banked by steep, wooded slopes — the tranquil ponds resemble miniature versions of the glacial "kettles" found in northern states.

But pretty names like "Kettle Moraine" aren't used to describe the jewels of southeast Kansas.

The ponds are called strip pits.

Maybe the folks in Crawford and Cherokee Counties don't want outsiders attracted to their favorite fishing holes?

"Strip pit falls in the same category as trash dump — but it's a beautiful area," said Mike Cox, information chief, Department of Wildlife and Parks.

In an effort to escape the less-than-lovely connotations of the term pit, the state now uses the name Mined Land Wildlife Area for the 250 public ponds it manages in the area.

But there are at least as many strip mine ponds on private lands. And the people who fish them are sure to continue calling them "Washing Machine Pit" or "Island Pit," in reference to some distinguishing trait, such as a discarded Maytag rusting away on the bank.

Dug by coal companies, the pits began as scars on the landscape. After the steamshovels left, waters trickled in and trees and flowers returned. Some of the ponds were donated to the state, others remained in private hands. Most, if not all, were stocked with largemouth bass, channel cats and panfish.

Small flat-bottomed boats or canoes are ideal for fishing the pits. Bass grow large in the ponds, even though their habitat often is confined to the shallow edges, since the pits typically drop off quickly to depths of 30 or 40 feet.

Because of the limited habitat, strip pits can be overfished. Each year, Wildlife and Parks rests two of its 45 mined-area sections by closing their waters to fishing.

Spotted bass, crappie and bluegill can be found in many of the pits; wipers and walleye have been introduced to a few of the larger ones.

There's no health hazard in eating fish from the mine waters "as far as we know," said district fisheries biologist Rob Frigerri.

Oxidized iron released from broken rocks tints some of the ponds with a rusty tinge. Iron dust can smother eggs and invertebrates as it settles in outlet streams, Frigerri said.

Of greater concern, he said, is the sulfur exposed by miners' shovels. "It mixes with air and water to form sulfuric acid," Frigerri said.

The process can sterilize a strip pit in the same way that acid rain is believed to have killed fish and invertebrate life in many lakes of the Northeast. Wildlife and Parks has used lime to reduce acidity in a few pit ponds.

"Out of 250 lakes, we might have a history of problems in 25," Frigerri said.

Because of their kettle shape and high banks, strip pits get very hot in summertime. Bring plenty of fluids to drink and try to time your trip to the pits for spring, fall, early mornings or late evenings.

Maps and brochures of public strip pits are available from Kansas Department of Wildlife and Parks, Pittsburg Office, Rt. 2, Box 372 AAA, Pittsburg, Kansas 66726.

26. **Montgomery** (H-13). Channel cats, largemouth bass, crappie and bluegill are caught in this 105-acre lake, surrounded by 1,300 acres of land, four miles southeast of Independence. Swimming, boat rentals and concessions are available.

27. **Nebo** (B-13). Largemouth bass, channel cats and bluegill can be found among the bullhead and carp at this 38-acre lake about eight miles east of Holton.

28. **Neosho** (G-14). Channel catfish, walleye and panfish have been stocked in this 92-acre lake five miles north and three miles east of Parsons.

29. **Osage** (D-13). A 140-acre lake 4 miles outside of Carbondale, Osage is stocked with largemouth, channel cats, bluegill and sunfish. Concessions are available.

30. **Ottawa** (C-10). This 138-acre lake, six miles northeast of Bennington, features a swimming beach in addition to the usual rough camping, picnic areas and drinking water. Largemouth bass, channel cats, bluegill and rough fish swim here.

31. **Pottawatomie Number One** (B-12). Very small at 24 acres, this lake five miles north of Westmoreland offers fishing for channel cats, largemouth and bluegill. Over 160 acres of public land surround the lake.

32. **Pottawatomie Number Two** (C-12). Boat rentals are available at this 75-acre lake 1½ miles east and 2½ miles north of Manhattan. Concessions, camping and picnic areas can also be found on the 173 acres of public land around the lake. It's a nice spot to fish for crappie, bluegill and other panfish.

33. **Rooks** (B-6). Sometimes dry, like most

smaller lakes in northwest Kansas, Rooks is known to support channel cat, walleye and bass when wet. It's located 2½ miles south and 2 miles west of Stockton. Rooks' 67-acre basin is encircled by another 246 acres of state land.

34. **Saline** (D-9). A 39-acre pool 2½ miles north and 2 miles west of Salina, this lake supports channel cats, panfish and largemouth bass. Another 39 acres of state land lies adjacent to the basin.

35. **Scott** (D-3). A gorgeous wooded camping area 12 miles north of Scott City, Lake Scott is not technically a fishing lake, but a State Park, although its 115 acres of water are managed by Wildlife and Parks fisheries biologists.

Lake Scott offers a swimming beach, concessions building and some of the finest campsites in western Kansas. Largemouth bass swim among the stumps and snags of the lake's western shore; fishing also is good for bass, crappie and catfish in the stream channel at the bottom of the lake. Channel cats and walleye have been stocked in Scott as well.

Rainbow trout — stocked for viewing, not catching — swim in the cool waters of the Big Springs Nature Area, which features a nature trail.

The park also features the only known Indian pueblo ruin in Kansas. El Cuartelejo was built by a mixed band of Apache and Taos Indians in the mid-1600s.

36. **Shawnee** (C-13). Largemouth bass, channel cats, crappie and bluegill can be found in 135-acre Shawnee Lake. Seven miles north and 2½ miles east of Silver Lake, Shawnee is surrounded by nearly 500 acres of state land.

37. **Sheridan** (B-4). An 87-acre lake 11 miles east of Hoxie, Sheridan harbors largemouth bass, crappie, channel cats and walleye. Camping, picnic areas and drinking water available on the surrounding 256 acres.

38. **Sherman** (C-1). A large 225-acre basin, Sherman often lies dry. Call the Department of Wildlife and Parks at (316) 672-5911 in advance for information about whether the basin is holding water and fish.

39. **Washington** (A-11). Crappie, bluegill, channel catfish and largemouth bass can be found in this 111-acre lake. Camping, drinking water and picnic areas are available on 350 acres of public land seven miles north and three miles west of the town of Washington.

40. **Wilson** (F-14). A 120-acre lake in southeast Kansas, 1½ miles southeast of Buffalo, Wilson harbors largemouth bass, channel cats, bluegill, crappie, catfish and flatheads. Fishing is best in spring and fall, or on cool nights during the hot summer months. Camping, drinking water and picnic areas are available.

41. **Woodson** (F-13). Just five miles east of Toronto, Woodson can be combined with Fall River and Toronto Reservoirs in a single day's search for fishing hot spots. Largemouth bass, crappie, channel cats and panfish reside in the 179-acre lake, surrounded by 250 acres of state land. Boat rentals are available, in addition to camping, picnic areas and water.

TOWN AND COUNTRY LAKES
Some of the nicest places in Kansas to wet a fishing line, pitch a tent or spread a picnic blanket can be found at the dozens of locally owned and managed lakes across the state.

Developed by cities, towns and counties, the lakes typically feature concessions stands, bait shops, campgrounds, picnic shelters and sandy swimming beaches.

A few of the tree-lined community lakes, such as Council Grove and Eureka, are surrounded by stretches of private property and ringed with summer cabins. This is rare in Kansas, where land around major reservoirs is owned by the government and managed for flood control and wildlife.

Special permits are required to help

cover the costs of managing community lakes and associated parks. Separate fees often are charged for fishing and boating. Nonresidents pay more than locals at most lakes. In a very few cases, such as Wellington's city lakes, nonresidents may only fish in the company of residents.

Similar in size to state fishing lakes, community lakes are rarely managed specifically for anglers. These are multipurpose waters, where waterski boats zoom around in patterns designed to leave some room for fishermen.

A state biologist often manages the community lake's fishery, which can change dramatically from year to year because of small size. Biologists rarely have the freedom to completely overhaul a lake by draining it and starting over. However, such management techniques appear to be unnecessary at many lakes, which offer excellent fishing opportunities year after year.

For seasonal updates on a specific lake, call the regional Wildlife and Parks office and ask them to put you in touch with the biologist responsible for the waters you plan to fish.

Every list of state community lakes differs somewhat in how they group clusters of small ponds and in which lakes are omitted for being too small, too dry or too obscure. This list includes some little ones and some obscure ones, but there still may be a hidden hole or two that escaped it.

1. **Afton Lake** (G-10). A popular spot 12 miles west of Wichita, Lake Afton is best known for its channel and flathead catfish. Feeders attract the fish to specific locations within casting distance of shore at regular intervals, but you can't keep channel cats under 16 inches. A few largemouth over the 15-inch limit are present. Carp fishing is phenomenal around fish feeders once the water temperature hits 70 degrees. Walleye and wipers have been stocked in recent years, but aren't numerous.

2. **Alma City Lake** (C-12). A 90-acre lake stocked with channel catfish, bluegills, largemouth, walleye and green sunfish, three miles southeast of Alma.

3. **Altamont City Lake** (H-14). A tiny lake, a few miles south of Altamont, with largemouth, panfish and channel cats.

4. **Anthony City Lake** (H-9). a nice sized 156-acre lake with channel cats, largemouth, crappie, bluegill and sunfish, one mile north and ½ mile west of Anthony.

5. **Atchison County Watershed Lakes** (B-14). Crappie, channel catfish, largemouth bass, bluegill and a few walleye swim in these lakes, four miles north and two miles west of Atchison.

6. **Atwood Lake** (A-2). Little more than a mud hole for many years, this lake in the northwest corner of Kansas was recently renovated by local citizens in cooperation with the state. The shallow end of the divided lake offers excellent largemouth bass habitat, but there have been problems on the deeper side with seepage of precious water where enthusiastic dozer operators dug a bit too deep. The lake also supports crappie, channel catfish and panfish. Its renovation was inspired, in part, by an old graduate thesis written by the town's most famous son: former Governor Mike Hayden.

7. **Belleville Lake (Rocky Pond)** (A-10). A 20-acre lake on East 12th Street, Belleville harbors crappie, carp, channel cats and bullhead.

8. **Blue Mound City Lake** (E-15). A 19-acre lake with channel catfish, largemouth bass, bluegill and crappie, one mile west and one mile north of Blue Mound.

9. **Bourbon County Lake (Elm Creek)** (F-15). Spotted and largemouth bass share this gorgeous 106-acre lake, two miles north of Hiattville. After a long period of high rainfall and turbidity, the spotted bass seem to outnumber the largemouth, but after a few years of moderate rainfall, the largemouth get the upper hand. A small number of large walleye remain in

the lake, where they reproduce naturally. Fishing also is good for crappie and bluegill.

10. Carbondale City Lake (D-13). A big community lake at 200 acres, Carbondale boasts a large variety of species, including largemouth bass, white bass, channel catfish, bluegill, crappie, flatheads and green sunfish. It lies three miles east of Carbondale.

11. Chanute City Lake (F-14). Largemouth, channel cats, bluegill and crappie stock this 77-acre lake on the south edge of Chanute.

12. Council Grove City Lake (D-12). A big, beautiful lake ringed with cabins and tall trees, Council Grove City Lake lies a short walk from the reservoir that shares its name. Walleye and wiper numbers are higher in the 434-acre city lake than in the reservoir. Largemouth bass, spotted bass, channel cats and crappie also live here.

13. Coldwater City Lake (H-6). The pride of Coldwater boasts wipers, walleye, largemouth bass, white bass and crappie, plus beautifully maintained camping, picnic and swimming areas.

14. Empire Lake (H-15). Smallmouth bass, spotted bass and largemouth are all native to the spectacular streams that feed this 120-acre lake in the southeast corner of the state. Other species include: crappie, white bass, channel and flathead catfish, bluegill and sunfish. Boat rentals are available.

15. Eureka City Lake (F-12). A home to lunker largemouth bass, this pretty 259-acre lake was developed by the Civilian Conservation Corps in the 1930s. Willows shade the shallows of this cabin-ringed lake, where a day of nonresident fishing cost only $1 in 1990. Spotted bass, channel and flathead catfish, crappie and sunfish also roam Eureka Lake.

16. Ford County Lake (G-5). Just northeast of Dodge City, this 17-acre lake features channel cats, crappie, largemouth bass, sunfish and carp.

17. Fort Riley Ponds (C-11). The public can fish on many stocked ponds in the military reservation most of the year, though areas are closed from time to time due to maneuvers. Some ponds at the Fort, north of Junction City, are stocked with trout, northern pike and spotted bass. Others hold largemouth bass, channel catfish and panfish. For more information, contact the Fort Riley Natural Resources Office, (913) 239-6669.

18. Fort Scott City Lakes (F-15). The entrance to two lakes lies two miles south and three miles west of Fort Scott. A healthy population of largemouth bass, a fair number of large, adult walleye, white bass, channel catfish, bluegill and green sunfish swim in Lake Fort Scott, by far the larger of the two at 352 acres. Channel cats, bass, bluegill, crappie and sunfish can also be caught in the 75-acre Rock Creek Lake.

19. Gardner City Lakes (D-15). Channel and flathead catfish, crappie, bluegill, panfish and largemouth bass have been stocked in this small lake north of Gardner.

20. Garnett City Lakes (E-14). Largemouth, channel catfish, crappie, redear sunfish and other panfish live in two small lakes, one on the north side of town, the other on the south.

21. Gridley City Lakes (E-13). Channel catfish are the major attraction to this 25-acre lake, ½ mile east and ¾ mile north of Gridley. Largemouth bass and panfish can also be caught here.

22. Harvey County East Lake (F-10). Just 30 minutes from Wichita, Harvey County East Lake offers good bass fishing and more. It features a swimming beach, picnic pavilions, 115 campsites with electricity, public hunting areas, superb birdwatching opportunities and a water-skiing route designed to prevent conflicts between recreational boaters and fishermen. The lake offers 16 jetties for shore fishing. Crappie and carp also thrive among the flooded timber, cattails and brushpiles.

23. **Harvey County West Lake** (F-10). It's not a place to catch a stringer full of fish, but Harvey County West Lake may be the most perfect place in Kansas to bring the family for a relaxing day or weekend outdoors. A pool in the Little Arkansas River, the lake is loaded with small panfish, which can be fun for kids and fly fishermen to catch. Tall, thick-trunked trees shade the campgrounds. Bait and gear can be purchased at the park office. There's a separate swimming pond and three miles of nature trails.

24. **Herington City Lake** (D-11). Herington supports a thriving population of largemouth bass, kept healthy, in part, by a strong catch-and-release ethic among local anglers. Crappie, bluegill and channel cats also roam the lake.

25. **Hiawatha Municipal Lake** (A-14). Channel cats, largemouth bass and bluegill stock the lake.

26. **Holton City Lake (Prairie Lake)** (B-13). A 78-acre lake with channel cats, largemouth bass, crappie and bluegill.

27. **Horton City Lake (Mission Lake)** (A-14). A 175-acre lake with largemouth bass, bluegill, channel catfish, crappie, bullhead and carp.

28. **Jones Youth Recreation Park** (E-12). Spotted and largemouth bass make this an excellent fishing lake. Crappie, panfish and channel cats are also present.

29. **Kansas City Lakes** (C-15). Many city and county parks in the Kansas City area include small lakes with public fishing opportunities. One of the largest is 332-acre Wyandotte County Lake, off Wolcott Drive on the northwest side of the city. Largemouth bass, channel catfish, crappie, bluegill, carp, bullhead and northern pike have been stocked here. Channel catfish, bullhead and bluegill are common in virtually all of the urban lakes.

30. **Lansing City Lake** (C-15). A small, urban lake stocked with bluegill, catfish and bass.

31. **Leavenworth Lake (Jerry's)** (B-14). A small, metropolitan lake with some channel catfish, bass and bluegill.

32. **Lebo City Lake** (E-13). A 78-acre lake with largemouth bass, channel catfish, crappie, bluegill, white bass and carp.

33. **Lenexa Lake (Rose's)** (C-15). A small, urban lake with bluegill, catfish and some bass.

34. **Logan City Lake** (A-6). A small lake, four miles south of Logan, with channel cats, largemouth bass, bluegill, crappie and a few walleye.

35. **Lone Star Lake** (C-14). A 200-acre impoundment with concessions, boat rentals and other facilities, Lone Star lies 15 miles southwest of Lawrence and was recently renovated. Channel catfish between 12 and 16 inches thrive in the lake, which also holds crappie, largemouth bass and bluegill.

36. **Louisburg Lake** (D-15). A new, combination state and community lake, with bass, channel catfish, crappie and bluegill. Wipers may be a fish of the future in this 240-acre lake, where the fishing is free but the shorelines are managed by the city.

37. **Madison City Lake** (F-12). A 97-acre lake, two miles south and ½ mile west of Madison, with largemouth bass, channel catfish and panfish.

38. **Marion County Lake** (E-11). A lovely lake built by the Civilian Conservation Corps, Marion County Lake yielded the state record spotted bass — 4 pounds, 7 ounces — back in 1977, and many local anglers believe the next spotted bass record will come from Marion as well. A spring-fed, 153-acre lake, Marion is 40 feet deep near the dam and features some steep dropoffs. A heated fishing dock is open year-round near the park office and bait shop. Crappie, walleye and channel catfish are also present. For current updates, call the park office at (316) 382-3240.

39. **Moline City Lakes** (G-12). Three small lakes on the outskirts of Moline harbor channel catfish, largemouth bass, crappie and bluegill.

40. **Mound City Lake** (E-15). Built much like Hillsdale Reservoir, with loads of creek channel and flooded timber, Mound City supports good numbers of largemouth bass, channel catfish, crappie and bluegill. A 12-to-18-inch slot length limit applies on largemouth bass. There are also length and creel limits on crappie and bluegill, unlike most lakes.

41. **North Park Lake** (C-15). A small urban lake with bluegill, channel cats and bass.

42. **Ogden City Lake** (C-11). A small lake with bluegill, crappie, channel cats, bass and bullhead.

43. **Olatha Lakes** (D-15). Led by 170-acre city lake on west side of town, Olathe also offers public fishing in several small park lakes and ponds. Largemouth bass, bluegill, channel catfish, crappie, walleye, white bass, sunfish and carp are present.

44. **Olpe City Lake** (E-12). A 90-acre lake on southwest side of Olpe with limited numbers of largemouth bass, spotted bass, channel catfish, bluegill and bullhead.

45. **Osage City Lake** (D-13). A 50-acre lake just south of Osage City, with channel catfish, bullhead, largemouth bass, bluegill and crappie.

46. **Osawatomie City Lake** (D-15). A very small lake three miles northwest of town with channel catfish, largemouth bass, crappie, bluegill, bullhead and sunfish.

47. **Overland Park Lakes** (C-15). Several small city park lakes with bluegill, sunfish and channel catfish.

48. **Paola City Lake** (D-15). A big, 220-acre lake 1½ miles northeast of Paola, with channel catfish, largemouth bass, crappie, bluegill, sunfish, bullhead and carp.

49. **Parker City Lake** (E-15). A farm-pond sized basin southwest of Parker, with bass, bluegill, channel catfish and sunfish.

50. **Parsons City Lake** (G-14). A very large impoundment of nearly 1,000 acres, four miles north and 3½ miles west of Parsons. Largemouth bass, channel and flathead catfish, bluegill, crappie, bullhead and carp are present.

51. **Plainville Township Lake** (C-6). A 158-acre lake, two miles west of Plainville, with channel catfish, largemouth bass, crappie, bluegill and bullhead.

52. **Pleasanton City** (E-15). By far the largest and most fished of three lakes in Pleasanton, the 92-acre East City Lake supports largemouth bass, channel catfish and so many crappie that their growth is stunted. Wipers and walleye have been stocked recently and should provide superb catch-and-release fishing in years to come.

53. **Pratt County Lake** (G-7). A 96-acre lake located 3 miles east and 1 mile south of Pratt, with good numbers of fast-growing wipers, plus some channel catfish, bullhead, crappie, carp and sunfish.

54. **Prescott City Lake** (E-15). A small lake southeast of Prescott with bluegill, largemouth bass, sunfish, channel catfish and bullhead.

55. **Richmond City Lake** (E-14). A 20-acre lake with largemouth bass, crappie, channel catfish, bluegill, flathead catfish and sunfish. The lake lies 1 miles south and 1½ miles east of Richmond.

56. **Sabetha City Lake** (A-13). A good crappie lake of 140 acres, five miles west of Sabetha. Largemouth bass, channel catfish, sunfish and carp are present.

57. **Salina Lake (Lakewood)** (D-10). A 45-acre lake in north Salina with largemouth bass, crappie, channel catfish, bluegill, bullhead and carp.

58. **Scranton City Lake** (D-13). A small lake with bluegill and catfish.

59. **Sedan City Lakes** (H-12). The newer of two lakes is also the larger, at 75 acres, and lies 2½ miles northwest of Sedan. It features largemouth bass, spotted bass, channel catfish, bluegill, crappie and sunfish. The old lake, of 55 acres, remains 3 miles north of town. Largemouth, channel catfish, bluegill, spotted bass and sunfish range here as well.

60. **Sedgwick County Ponds** (G-10). A trio of ponds awaits anglers at Sedgwick

County Park, on the west side of Wichita, adjacent to the Zoo. Heavily stocked with rainbow trout during cool months for put-and-take fishing, the small lakes also receive frequent stockings of channel catfish, panfish and largemouth bass. Best fishing is in the kids' pond, but Dads aren't supposed to play there.

61. Shawnee Mission Lake (C-15). A 135-acre urban lake on southwest side of Shawnee Mission, run by Johnson County. Largemouth bass, bluegill, channel catfish and sunfish are present.

62. Spring Hill City Lake (D-15). A small lake with catfish, bluegill and some bass.

63. Sterling City Lake (E-8). A 25-acre lake, on the southeast edge of Sterling, with channel cats, bluegill and a few largemouth bass.

64. Topeka Lakes (C-14). Lake Shawnee, on the east edge of town, holds a limited supply of largemouth bass, channel catfish, bluegill, crappie, walleye, sunfish and white bass in its 410 acres. A bass pond on the grounds of Cedar Crest, the Governor's residence, also is open for public fishing.

65. Thayer City Lake (G-14). A 25-acre lake, just southwest of Thayer, with largemouth bass, channel catfish, crappie and sunfish.

66. Wabaunsee County Lake (D-12). A 278-acre lake, five miles west of Eskridge, with many amenities. Largemouth bass, channel catfish, crappie, bluegill, walleye and flatheads are present.

67. Wamegho City Lake (C-12) A small lake with some bluegill, channel catfish and largemouth bass.

68. Watson Park Lake (G-10) A small lake off the Arkansas River in central Wichita, Watson is frequently stocked with put-and-take trout and channel catfish. A thriving bluegill population manages to maintain itself despite the fishing pressure, and carp are abundant.

69. Wellington City Lakes (G-10). Hargis Creek Lake, in northeast Wellington, features excellent crappie fishing in cycles. However, non-residents must be accompanied by residents who possess an annual fishing license. The same rules apply for the larger city lake 5 miles west and 1½ south of Wellington. Largemouth bass, crappie, channel and flathead catfish, sunfish and carp swim in the 349-acre lake.

70. Winfield City Lake (G-11). Approaching the size of a major reservoir at 1,200 acres, Winfield City Lake actually lies 9 miles north and 5 miles east of its namesake town. A consistently good lake for channel catfish, Winfield's crappie population has bounced back in recent years, though crappie are a cyclical species. Winfield also boasts a fair walleye population and plenty of mudflats for June drift fishing.

Index

George Stanley explored the four corners of Kansas as a hunter, fisherman and amateur naturalist while covering the outdoors beat for *The Wichita Eagle*. He has received first-place writing awards from the Outdoor Writers Association of America for magazine and newspaper stories about hunting, fishing, conservation and outdoor ethics. A special newspaper section he produced about the Great Outdoors of Kansas was honored as one of the nation's 10 best by the Associated Press Sports Editors Association. Stanley's special report on the 1988 forest fires at Yellowstone National Park made it to the semifinals of the prestigious Pulitzer competition.

In 1987, Stanley was named Outdoor Communicator of the Year by the Kansas Wildlife Federation for his aggressive, in-depth coverage of conservation issues in the state.

Stanley's hunting, fishing, humor and conservation articles have appeared in a number of national magazines, including *Sports Afield* and *Ducks Unlimited*, where he was a senior staff writer from 1980 to 1986.

The typefaces used in *Watermark Guide to Fishing in Kansas* are Centaur and Gill Sans. Both are translations of the original typefaces rendered digitally for the personal computer.

The main text face, Centaur, was designed by Bruce Rogers, considered by historians to be America's foremost book designer. Centaur takes its name from the book designed by Rogers in which it was first used, a limited edition of Maurice de Guérin's *The Centaur*, in 1915. Rogers later utilized Centaur to stunning effect in what is regarded as a masterpiece of typography, the Lectern Bible of the Oxford University Press, in 1935.

Gill Sans, used in this book primarily as a counterpoint face, was designed by Eric Gill and produced by the Monotype Corporation in 1928. Gill, a lapidary artist and sculptor, found inspiration for Gill Sans in the signage for the London Underground transit system. The transit lettering, designed by Gill's calligraphy teacher, Edward Johnston, was appreciated for its legibility. Gill produced a whole family of typefaces based on the letters. Typographers consider Gill Sans to be a clean, well-proportioned, and highly legible face.